WOMAN OF PURPOSE
Series

INVESTING
YOUR LIFE
IN THINGS
THAT MATTER

Linda McGinn Waterman

Pleasant W●rd
A Division of WINEPRESS PUBLISHING

Packaged by Pleasant Word, a division of WinePress Publishing, PO Box 428, Enumclaw, WA 98022. The views expressed or implied in this work do not necessarily reflect those of Pleasant Word, a division of WinePress Publishing. The author is ultimately responsible for the design, content and editorial accuracy of this work.

Scriptures are taken from the Holy Bible, New International Version, Copyright © 1973, 1978, 1984 by the International Bible Society, used by permission of Zondervan Publishing House; The Amplified Bible, Old Testament, © 1965 and 1987 by The Zondervan Corporation, The Amplified New Testament, © 1954, 1958, 1987 by The Lockman Foundation, used by permission; The Message Bible © 1993 by Eugene N. Peterson, NavPress, POB 35001, Colorado Springs, CO 80935, 4th printing in USA 1994, published in association with the literary agency—Aline Comm. POB 49068, Colorado Springs, CO 80949, used by permission; J. B. Phillips: The New Testament in Modern English, Revised Edition. © J. B. Phillips 1958, 1960, 1972, used by permission of Macmillan Publishing Company.

ISBN 1-4141-0164-3
Library of Congress Catalog Card Number: 2004103841

Dedicated to T. R. Hollingsworth
whose research assistance, consultation, editing, diligent labor,
and companionship made this book possible.
She is not only a tremendous writing partner but my mother
and dear friend.

———————

CONTENTS

ACKNOWLEDGMENTS

*My appreciation goes to Reen, Ruthie, John, Amy, and Sarah,
my precious family, for their loving support and consistent
encouragement and to my Lord Jesus Christ who makes
impossible things possible by His power.*

INTRODUCTION

*B*orn only to die. That appeared to be my lot. After ten years awaiting conception, I came to be. My parents anticipated my birth with joy. Only hours after I arrived, the doctors informed my parents that death was inevitable. Due to an undiagnosed Rh negative blood problem, I had only hours to live. I was so jaundiced, my prognosis was hopeless.

My parents prayed, dedicating this long anticipated baby to God. If He were to save her life, she was His completely. The Arlington hospital decided to use me as a guinea pig. With my parents' permission they would attempt a never-before-performed complete blood exchange transfusion. They did. It worked.

My earliest memories are of my mother's words, "You must find out who this God is and what His purposes are for your life." These two pursuits shaped my life.

As a teenager I often lay in bed at night asking myself the questions, "Who is God?" and "What is eternally significant?" When, at eighteen, I came to realize I could know God through an actual relationship with His Son I entered into that relationship with abandon. Nothing else had satisfied the aching need for fulfillment and relief from the emptiness within. Finding the answer to the second question became my life mission. So it is with delight I disclose to you the results of my pursuits, the discoveries of my life.

How do you invest your life in things that matter? We are each given the same priceless commodity—life. One life to live. How we spend those precious moments, we alone determine. Yes, outside factors, events, and circumstances play their part, but ultimately the choices are ours.

This book is focused on investment. Today when you think about investment, money may be the first thing that comes to mind. "Money," the managing editor of *MONEY* magazine said, "has become the new sex in this country."[1] Money has become America's number-one obsession, writes another. Yet, while financial management dominates our lives, our investment in life itself—of far greater importance—often remains unexplored.

Jesus tells us, "Do not store up for yourselves treasures on earth, where moth and rust destroy, and where thieves break in and steal. But store up for yourselves treasures in heaven, where moth and rust do not destroy, and where thieves do not break in and steal. For where your treasure is, there your heart will be also" (Matt. 6:19–21).

Marketing experts develop elaborate schemes to convince us that investment in their latest project, product, or program is essential. Is it? The urgencies of daily life leave little time for examination of our investment in living. Many of us rarely look to the future to develop long-range strategies for the investment of our lives.

The fact that you picked up this book expresses your desire to invest your life in ways that reap more than temporal benefit—that produce eternal dividends. You want to feel your daily investment of time, money, and energy in life's activities results in the creation of something of lasting value. This, too, is my desire.

My desire is that Jesus' words will be yours when the game of life ends and you face the Heavenly Father, "'I have brought you glory on earth by completing the work you gave me to do'" (John 17:4). It is my belief that the following verse is profoundly true:

> Just think, you're not here by chance,
>   but by God's choosing.
> His hand formed you and made you
>   the person you are.
> He compares you to no one else—
>   you are one of a kind.
> You lack nothing that His grace
>   can't give you.
> He has allowed you to be here
>   at this time in history to fulfill
>   His special purpose for this generation.
> How thankful I am that He has allowed me to be here
>   at the same time you are!

AUTHOR UNKNOWN

Each of us has been born "for such a time as this" (Esther 4:14), and though we may see our contribution as small, the sheer joy of fulfilling God's will for our lives, and investing our time, money, and energy in the things He has specifically designed for us, has eternal repercussions and may yield eternal dividends beyond our imagination.

This book describes the results of my pilgrimage. Won't you join me? Learn with me how to grasp perspective on life, discover new aspects of God's character, experience fresh glimpses of His love. And while doing so, discover the mysteries of investing your life in things that transcend the limits of time and stretch into eternity.

Don't be afraid. Join me in applying God's Word to every aspect of your life, guided and directed by His Holy Spirit as your teacher. Begin your pilgrimage today. Go deeper with God. He will meet the deepest needs of your heart. Only He can.

PART ONE

Thinking Sharp

for Effective

Investment

What did you do last month . . . or last Saturday . . . or yesterday? Can you remember? Or have your days blurred into a frantic flurry of activity soon forgotten, moments devoid of memories.

Each of us is investing our lives, ourselves, in something every-day. The clock of life ticks on—days, weeks, months invested in things of either lasting significance or worthless pursuit.

When you look back years, even decades from now, what amidst all your hectic activities will have produced dividends that count?

Approaching my fortieth birthday, I began to ask myself the same questions posed here. I decided to reevaluate my life and in doing so transformed it. Things that had been so important before lessened in value. Balance grew out of chaos. I examined my opinions and convictions—clutched protectively—in the light of God's Word and found some of them were faulty. In summary, my investments shifted and the resulting peace is indescribable.

I won't tell you it is easy. Ruts are hard to climb out of. Continuing in a well-worn path becomes easy even if you're going in the wrong direction. Investments are the same. They grow comfortable. We grow complacent. Before we know it, we forget to reevaluate our investments and make necessary changes. Our time, energy, and values flitter away never to be recovered just like money slipping through open fingers lost along the path of life.

So how do you invest in things that matter? First you must discover what matters. Since we want our life investment to last for eternity, we must ask ourselves what, in all that we do each day, will transcend time into eternity? What lasts for eternity? There are only two things. The Word of God hidden in our hearts and the people that go to heaven with us.

That scaled down your priorities. Right? God's Word and people are the only things that last for eternity, so only in them can we make an eternal investment. How do we do it? That's the question addressed throughout this book. This first section will look at the first area of investment, investing our lives in God's Word. Join me now as we discover how to invest our lives in things that matter by investing our lives in God's character and His Word.

Plotting Your Personal Investment Pilgrimage

*Are you ever in situations when you simply don't know
the right thing to do? How do you evaluate your choices?
How do you make a decision?
This chapter helps you begin to evaluate your choices
so that you can make choices that consistently invest your life
in things that matter.*

All Scripture is God-breathed and is useful for teaching,
rebuking, correcting and training in righteousness,
so that the man [or woman] of God may be thoroughly
equipped for every good work.

2 Timothy 3:16

Several years ago, my life changed. I had an encounter that altered my perspective. It was a simple series of events. Others would have thought nothing of it, but it became a turning point in my life that changed my perspective about everything. Let me tell you the story.

"Hi! Don't you pass by here almost every morning?" questioned the drive-through attendant with a grin.

"Yes. About every morning on my way to work," I answered with a smile. "Two cinnamon raisin biscuits and a medium Dr. Pepper with very little ice," I quipped in sing-song repetition. She giggled.

"Where do you work?"

"Downtown."

She tilted her head quizzically, "Oh, and what do you do?"

I felt myself tense. *Oh boy, here we go. How do I answer?* Speak at Christian conferences? Write Christian books? Teach Bible studies? The pause became uncomfortable.

"Write books," I answered weakly.

A surprised, "Write books?" Obviously she was searching for a suitable response.

I was ready to move on now. We could close this conversation. Any more questions might push me into a vulnerable position. *Lord, do I have to do this?* flashed through my brain.

"What kind of books?" Her animated face showed her interest.

"Books for women, mostly." *OK, Lord,* I thought. *I know I'm hedging.* "Christian books." There, I'd said it. Let the chips fall where they may. I sighed deeply.

"Now that's interesting," she said. "My husband and I were just discussing church last night. We haven't been to church in years.

But we've talked about going somewhere this Sunday. You got any suggestions?"

"Well, my husband is the pastor at the stone church just down the street. We'd love for you to come visit."

"Great! We'll see you on Sunday," she said.

A simple conversation at a fast-food drive-through was God's appointment for one couple to begin an exploration of the Christian life. God's methods constantly amaze me.

And it was God's appointment for me to begin to evaluate the teaching I had received from the Christian community. It had silently been impressed on me that people in the world were very closed to hearing about Jesus Christ and the Gospel. Accepting that assumption without questioning it, I felt different from the people I interacted with each day at the grocery store, cleaners, my children's school, and the golf course. Without realizing it, I became isolated from the secular world.

I would talk "to" those who did not know Christ, but not "with" them because I thought we had nothing in common. They wouldn't want to hear what I had to say anyway.

As a result of that drive-through encounter, I began to reevaluate my faith. I began to examine my attitudes, belief system, and ideas in light of God's Word in an attempt to discover if they were biblical or something imposed on me by well-meaning Christian authorities.

I'd like to introduce you to several friends of mine who have had similar struggles. Meet Susan, Jim, and Ellen.

Susan gazed aimlessly outside her picture window at the swaying trees in the brisk New England morning. The brilliant reds, yellows, and oranges of October's leaves held no beauty for her. All she could think about were her situation and the dilemma of her heart.

The pleasure she experienced last evening had been wonderful. But she had no peace within. Confusion tormented her. Words spoken privately to a friend haunted her.

"I really love Steve. He's such a wonderful Christian man. We never planned to get this involved, but I believe God sent Steve to me. It's His gift. Now I know what a Christian marriage should really be like.

"I've prayed and prayed Harry would become a Christian but he never changes. It's as if we don't live on the same planet. He doesn't understand my Christianity. We just don't connect. We don't communicate.

"When I'm with Steve it feels so right. I get to experience the Christian marriage that's missing with Harry. I don't want to leave Harry. He'd kill me if he ever found out. But I love Steve and can't seem to give him up."

Susan was imprisoned by guilt and misery as she relived that conversation. Deep within she knew she was wrong. But Steve was meeting her needs. How could she give him up?

Jim's head hung over his Bible as he prayed for direction from God. Something strange was happening in his church lately. He'd attended the mainline denominational church all his life. Things had been predictable, comfortable. Then the Holy Spirit came. That seemed the only way to describe it. Life gripped the church as new interest in God and His Word dominated conversation and activity. It got so that he couldn't wait to get to church himself. He, too, had prayed and asked God to fill Him daily with His Holy Spirit. He wanted to learn more about Jesus and be used by His Holy Spirit.

But lately things had changed. A new preacher moved into the community and developed a friendship with his pastor. Pastor Tom shared stories with him about the revival that recently swept through the congregation. The stranger began to attend services. Then "prayer counseling" began.

It sounded harmless enough. People with concerns and problems met with the stranger and a few church leaders to pray about their needs.

Jim's thoughts wandered to the day when he decided to seek prayer counseling as well. His daughter's rebellion and obstinance had worried him for some time. He thought he might get help.

When he entered the prayer counseling room, the stranger had seemed nice enough. Friends who were church leaders stood prepared to pray with him. But before Jim knew it, the stranger was interrogating him, asking him about his personal life. Then he began to accuse Jim of having a spirit of irritation, frustration, resentment, and bitterness toward his daughter. The stranger said these demons needed "casting out." Jim knew the Bible spoke of demons. He didn't know quite how to respond. So he went along. Nothing much happened, and the stranger looked disappointed that Jim didn't respond in the manner he expected. Everyone prayed, and the session was over.

Now several days later, it all seemed so strange. Were all these things—irritation, resentment, anger—really "demons" or were they merely sin in his life? Did he need exorcism or repentance? He wanted to agree with the stranger because his pastor obviously endorsed what the man was teaching, but was it all biblical?

Ellen sat across from Ann in Kathy's living room. Coffee perked rhythmically in the kitchen, its fragrance filling the air. Busily Kathy fixed pastry for them as she introduced Ann. "Ann has some questions she'd like to ask you, Ellen. Ann knows I don't know very much about Christ, but I know you do so I invited her over to meet you. Maybe you have some answers."

Ellen smiled and turned to Ann. "Ann, what are the questions you'd like to talk about? I certainly don't have all the answers, but I'll do my best to help out."

Ann shifted restlessly in her chair. "I've been in a relationship with this guy, Brian. I'm in the middle of a divorce, but I really like Brian. He hasn't called me lately. I want to know if God wants him to be in my life and if he's coming back. I've prayed and prayed but can't seem to get any answer from God. So a couple days ago I felt as if God was telling me to call the psychic hot line."

Ann's expression challenged Ellen. "I know sometimes these people are quacks, but don't tell me they don't know what they're talking about. This woman knew Brian's hair color, eye color, and even what profession he was in. I told Kathy about this, and she told me I should talk to you."

Ellen's thoughts raced. Silently she asked the Lord for guidance. She quickly searched for answers to Ann's questions. What does the Bible say about psychics? If they're wrong, why? How can they come up with accurate information at times?

Approaching God's Word with Questions

Each of these stories portray Christian people with real questions. I've known each of them and many more. As I listen to their stories I realize they are asking the same questions I ask myself every day: *What does the Bible really say? What is God's mind as He reveals Himself through His Word on each subject? What do I believe, and how, in this rapidly changing world, can He use me to communicate His truth to those around me?*

Why were Christians like Susan, Jim, and Ellen struggling for answers to difficult questions? Was their confusion the result of secular society's influence? Or could it be that they were not challenged to think biblically by the Christian community. They were robbed of the opportunity to discover God's answers for life's situations and in turn be strengthened with inner convictions that would hold in times of temptation and turmoil.

Raised in a Christian home and then called to full-time Christian ministry at age eighteen, I have spent my entire life looking at the world from within the cloistered walls of the Christian community. I, for the most part, fulfilled my role by adopting the attitudes and belief systems of my leaders and conforming to the expectations and demands of my peers.

Finally in 1993 I was asked to lead a seminar at a conference held in a university in the western Carolina mountains. It was an evangelism conference, and my topic was titled "Preparing Your Child for the 21st Century." As I began to study the upcoming century and to evaluate the Christian community as it faces the issues and concerns of those around them in the decade ahead, I began to examine all future aspects of our society from a biblical position.

My conclusion was that I and many others were running scared. We were scared of this huge, secular society that confronts us. Why?

Because we have been taught that being involved with the "world" will pollute us. We must avoid it at any cost. We do that by avoiding deep, personal relationships with non-Christians.

Secular Society through Christian Eyes

How many non-Christian friends do you have? I mean *real* friends. I was ashamed that it had become very easy for me to write Christian books, attend Christian conferences, listen to Christian radio, join in Christian church activities, and not speak to an unbeliever for days and even weeks. I created a cloistered commune that allowed me to only interact with my peers.

Maybe you are out in the secular world. You go to work every day and work constantly with non-Christians. But do you associate with them in a way that holds them at arms length, or do you get involved in their lives? How often do you offer to help with their problems or pray for their needs? There is another way we can isolate ourselves—through created distance.

During the last five years I have come to realize that non-Christians aren't different than we are. They feel joy, pain, suffering, and disillusionment. They hurt, laugh, and cry. The only thing that makes you or me different from the non-Christian is that we have Jesus Christ. He holds the key to every problem. Relationship with Him ensures that we are never alone. Jesus is the answer to life's concerns. Jesus.

In the following chapters, you will hear the results of Susan's, Ellen's, and Jim's stories. You will meet many others who will tell you the story of their pilgrimage into a deeper knowledge of God and His Word. *Pilgrimage* is the appropriate word. Pilgrimage best describes my experience as this book has developed. I will share the details of my pilgrimage from the prison of Christian isolation to the freedom of Christian participation with a world that is hurting and dying and in which many are lost.

I have come to believe that as we Christians begin to face the problems of our society, search for Biblical answers to the concerns that confront us, form convictions based not on what we have been told to think but on personal study of God's Word, we will begin to experience new freedom to invest our lives in things that really matter. Begin with me today.

SHARP THINKING IN A MUDDLED WORLD

Life is so daily.
Do you find it difficult to apply biblical thinking while making
everyday decisions? You can learn to apply Christian principles
more effectively when facing the hectic demands of life.

Do not conform any longer to the pattern of this world,
but be transformed by the renewing of your mind.
Then you will be able to test and approve what God's will is—his
good, pleasing and perfect will.

ROMANS 12:2

*K*evin's eyes glazed as he viewed the computer screen. How long had he been sitting there, staring? Lost in thought, he had no idea. Time passed unnoticed. Should he do it or not? Not *could* he do it. He was about to make one of the most important decisions of his life, and he was immobilized.

Kevin mentally reviewed his career. A top executive in his field of electrical engineering, he "had it all." A Virginia Military Institute graduate, he was quickly hired by a renowned Houston engineering construction firm. At twenty-one years old, he was senior project engineer supervising thirty others and pursuing his lifelong dream of making lots of money.

Four years later two men decided to build their own business. Their philosophy was to hire two hundred of the best in the field, pay them exorbitant salaries, give them anything they wanted and the opportunity to work on whatever they desired. The end result: everyone would walk away rich.

Selected as one of the two hundred, Kevin experienced success. The concept had worked. He was rich. Everything he had ever wanted in life was his. Then he became a Christian. The claims of Christ answered questions he had puzzled about all his life. He made his decision. He already knew that living with and for Jesus demanded a life change. He believed Jesus held the answers for all of life. But now this.

That morning, his boss walked into his office and disrupted his entire world. A new device had been discovered that would revolutionize their field. Only months earlier, a small businessman happened upon the device. Kevin's boss heard of it quite accidentally.

Now he wanted it. The boss outlined plans for Kevin to secretly pilfer plans for the device. Figuring the small businessman would sue, they saw little risk because it was known he didn't have the funds to win. What was Kevin to do? When Kevin hesitated, his boss made it clear that his job was on the line. He gave him twenty-four hours to think about it. If Kevin didn't agree, he could walk, his career destroyed.

What Really Matters?

Have you ever been placed in a situation where you were asked to do something you knew was wrong, and the consequences of refusing were monumental? What did you think? *Maybe it won't really matter if I do this once. Only one time, never again. The Lord will understand.*

Or did you come to God and pray? Did you say, *Lord, what's Your mind about this matter? What instructions do You want to give me through Your guidebook for life, the Bible?* Then did you turn to your Bible for answers?

Your answers to these questions are crucial when considering how to invest your life in things that matter. We must first identify what really matters. Does the application of God's Word in every situation really matter? Yes.

Why? Actually, we can answer that quite quickly by answering the fundamental question, What is eternal? What transcends time and can be taken with us to heaven when we die? There are two things noted earlier: the Word of God and the people who possess eternal life in Jesus Christ.

God's Word hidden in your heart through daily personal application will remain for eternity. The result of its application has eternal ramifications. Possibly as a result of God's Word applied in your heart and extended to them, people who believe in Jesus will be with you eternally in heaven.

Our priorities are quickly clarified. By first investing God's Word in our lives we are equipped to invest it in the lives of others. Kevin's question was valid. Does it matter that life's choices be consistently measured by the standard of God's Word? Yes. It matters.

What did Kevin do? He pulled his new Bible out of his desk drawer and turned to a passage his pastor covered the previous week: "Remind the people to be subject to rulers and authorities, to be obedient, to be ready to do whatever is good, . . ." (he paused at those words and thought for a minute) "to slander no one, to be peaceable and considerate, and to show true humility toward all men" (Titus 3:1–2).

He couldn't push aside childhood memories of learning the Ten Commandments in Sunday School when his parents took the time to drop him off at church. "Thou shalt not steal." He always thought the language strange, but he hadn't forgotten the verse. The point was unavoidable.

Kevin continued to study verses on the topic of stealing that he found in the concordance in the back of his Bible. He purposely read them in the context of the surrounding verses so that he wouldn't jump to false conclusions. Then he began to ask himself, *What is most consistent with the character of my God whom I have so recently come to love? What have I learned about His character during the brief time I've walked with Him?*

How do you handle the issues you face each day as you confront life in the real world? Do you find yourself in God's Word, prayerfully seeking God's guidance and help? Or do you immediately turn to others to tell you what to do?

I don't know about you, but sometimes when a crisis arises, I find myself asking others to pray before I've talked to God about the situation myself. I've come to realize that God wants me to read His Word and talk to Him first. Actually He wants me to talk with Him always. As I travel around the United States, I often ask those I address, "Do you talk to yourself?" First, there is silence. Then a few hands raise, and before you know it everyone is chuckling as their hands wave high in the air.

Everyone talks to himself. You're talking to yourself right now as you consider whether you agree with me. You're wondering where I'm going with this line of thinking.

We constantly carry on a personal conversation with ourselves. We evaluate every situation. We review conversations we've had with others over and over in our minds. We carry on an internal discussion about life and our evaluation of it.

I believe God wants us to invite Him into that conversation. That's what I believe Paul means when he tells the Thessalonians to "Pray without ceasing" (1 Thess. 5:17). God never gives us a command that we can't fulfill. So instead of talking to yourself, why not start talking with God?

PREPARING TO HEAR FROM GOD "IN THE WORD"

1. Confess all sin and ask to receive forgiveness, 1 John 1:9.
2. Pray to be filled with the Holy Spirit before reading God's Word, Ephesians 5:18.
3. Ask the Lord for wisdom and insight concerning your particular situation through your reading of His Word and sensitivity to His Spirit's direction, James 1:5.
4. Listen to God. His voice will never contradict His Word and He will give the wisdom and insight you need as you patiently trust and wait, Mark 9:7.
5. Thank Him for His care and guidance, Philippians 4:6–7.

Investing God's Word in Your Heart

"Christianly" thinking comes from taking the everyday events and situations of life—who we meet, what we hear on the radio, what we read in the newspaper, issues presented on television and movies—and discussing them with God, relying on His Word to give us direction in our thinking and responding. You can do that only if you read the Bible.

Listening to your pastor each Sunday morning and attending other church activities throughout the week, even listening to Christian radio all day long will never replace insights and wisdom God supplies as you talk with Him about your particular situation after reading His Word each day.

My daughter once said to me, "Mom, I'm not as spiritual as you are. I don't read my Bible every day. I am so busy in the morning I don't have time, and at night I'm too tired."

I replied, "Ruthie, I'm not so spiritual. I don't read my Bible every day because I think I have to be spiritual or because it's a Christian duty I have to perform. I read the Bible and spend time with God all day long because He's my best friend. I wouldn't survive without Him. Life is tough. I'm glad He loves me and wants to guide and direct my day as I trust Him. I wouldn't make it otherwise."

Is Jesus Christ your best friend? Do you know His love that meets the deepest needs of your heart, a love that no human being on earth could ever give you? If you don't, you can.

All you have to do is ask the Lord Jesus Christ to forgive your sin. You have sinned every time you have raised your hand defiantly to God saying "My way, not Yours."

Jesus died to take the penalty for your sin which is death. He gave His life so that you wouldn't have to. If you believe in His death and resurrection, you can spend eternity with God. That's what it means to become a Christian. There is no other way to have a relationship with God. God is perfect, holy, just, and can't even look at sin. He will not allow it into His heaven, His eternal home.

If you have unfinished business with God, why not stop right now and change your situation? Do you just know *about* God or do you really know Him? You can know Him. Pray this simple prayer:

Jesus,

I agree with You that I am a sinner. Forgive me for rebelling against You. I believe that You died on the cross to pay the penalty for my sin. Come into my life and change me. Please give me an intimate, dynamic relationship with You. Thank You for doing this for me and in me.

Amen.

If you prayed this prayer with sincerity, you have now begun your new life with Jesus Christ. Remember, relationships don't just happen. Good relationships are a result of commitment. Learning about God and what He desires for you comes with spending time with Him.

Here are some practical ways to start.

STEPS FOR APPLYING GOD'S TRUTH DAILY

1. Pray for wisdom to hear and recognize the Holy Spirit's teaching, John 14:26.
2. Study a concordance (an alphabetical listing of words in the Bible) for verses on a particular subject. This equips you to evaluate the "whole counsel of God" to arrive at balanced, biblical conclusions consistent with God's Word and character, Acts 20:27; 2 Timothy 3:16; Matthew 22:29. "Proof-texts" may use verses out of context, arriving at false conclusions which distort the meaning of God's Word.
3. Read commentaries for further insight. Suggested commentaries:
   Matthew Henry's Commentary
   William Hendriksen's, The New Testament Commentary
   Wycliffe Commentary
   Eerdman's Bible Commentary
   The Believer's Bible Commentary (N.T.)
   New International Commentary on the New Testament
   New American Commentary
4. Ask the Lord to equip you to apply His Word to your particular problems and situations, Hebrews 4:12; Ephesians 1:17–23.
5. After prayer, wait. Listen for God's answer. Be sensitive to the Holy Spirit's teaching and direction throughout your day in every situation with every person.
6. Thank God for His insight and wisdom.

Meeting God in His Word

As you grow in your relationship with God by reading His Word and talking with Him throughout your day, God will begin to help you think biblically. He will create a grid of truth in your mind and heart through which all of life's events will flow. It will not be a grid imposed on you by what other people think or design by the faulty ideas of a culture that is searching to know God, but a grid of truth.

God is truth. Jesus said clearly, "I am the way, the truth, the life. No one comes to the Father but through me" (John 14:6). When you meet those who do not know Christ, encourage them to search for truth in God's Word. They will always come face to face with God.

Unfortunately, in our society today we are not taught to think. We are given rules to follow, instructions to carry out, behavior to emulate, but thinking? Well, that's another issue that no one has time to address.

Stefan Ulstein writes in a *Christianity Today* article, "Critical thinking and spiritual reflection are harder to teach than mere tasks. But there are no short cuts that can substitute for careful reading and probing discussion. It is easier to teach a Sunday School lesson where kids just fill in the blanks than it is to nurture inquiring minds and questioning spirits."[1]

Many Christians flounder in their decision-making because the hard and fast rules that used to apply, the discipline for behavior that seemed so comfortable in a society based primarily on Christian principles, are in many cases no longer applicable to daily life. Issues we and our children face never touched the lives of our parents and grandparents. Previous mores and social prejudices don't fit contemporary life. Why? Because often they were not biblical nor did they flow from relationship with God consistent with His Word. They were simply the socially correct thing to do, traditions to be maintained.

Traditions can be wonderful. They can bring to mind important moments in our lives or hallmark significant events, but it is dangerous when they shape behavior. God is the shaper of humankind and He uses His Word, His Spirit, and His presence to accomplish the task.

Our challenge today as Christians is to search God's Word, discover His truth, which will always be consistent with His character, and apply it in the situations that confront us in contemporary culture.

We cannot depend on our pastor, TV personalities, or radio speakers to hold the substance of all truth. Only God holds truth, and He will reveal to us the manner in which we can apply His truth in our lives.

What did Kevin do in response to his boss's demands? First, after searching God's Word and deciding that it would be thievery to take the plans for the small businessman's device, he asked his Christian friends to pray as he prepared to give his boss an answer.

He went to his boss the next day and kindly explained to him what a negative impression this action would give their corporation. He suggested buying the small businessman's patent in hopes that future discoveries by the man would be presented to their corporation first, giving them a cutting edge in upcoming years. Kevin's boss was receptive to the suggestion and encouraged him to follow through on his idea.

Obviously, Kevin's situation turned out well for everyone involved. What if Kevin had been fired instead? Would he have made the correct decision? Yes. And because his desire was to please the Lord, God would have worked the situation out for Kevin's best.

Why? Because God is not so concerned about our situations as He is about us. His desire is that we be conformed to the image of His Son, and because He loves us He will use every event in our lives, negative and positive, to accomplish that purpose (Rom. 8:28–29). Only He knows what is good. After all, He is the originator and definer of "good." He is good and His character is good, so we can always trust Him to act in a way consistent with His character. He is not fickle. He is changeless. He and His Word can be trusted without exception.

CHAPTER THREE

What Do You Believe?
Are You Sure?

*Who or what directs your choices when life's situations
and events present challenges seemingly too great to bear?
What are the fundamentals of your belief systems?
What is right? What is wrong? How do you know?*

"Then you will know the truth,
and the truth will set you free."
JOHN 8:32

We see that investing your life in things that matter is possible when you first invest God's Word in your life. How can you do that?

Let's go back to Ellen and Ann whom we met in the last chapter. Remember Ellen's thoughts? Silently she asked the Lord for guidance and quickly searched for answers to Ann's questions: What does the Bible say about psychics? If they're wrong, why?

Ellen paused to respond to Ann's question. She knew instantly that God wouldn't tell Ann to call a psychic for direction. Why was she sure? After all, didn't God use Balaam's donkey to speak to Balaam? How could she know without doubt that Ann was not hearing from God? Ellen reminded herself of some of the facts she knew about God.

+ God never changes. He never does anything inconsistent with His Word or character, Hebrews 13:8.

+ God promises to give us wisdom if we ask. He'll do this without criticizing us for asking, James 1:5.

+ God acknowledges the presence of psychics but strictly forbids His children from participating with them. Any form of divination or occult activity is to be adamantly avoided, Deuteronomy 18:9–14; 1 Samuel 28; Galatians 5:20–21.

Because Ann mentioned that she had prayed, Ellen knew she recognized and desired God's guidance. Henry Blackaby and Claude King, in *Experiencing God,* wrote, "No one is going to seek God on his own initiative because God says, 'There is none who seeks God' (Rom. 3) and 'No one can come to Me [Jesus] unless the Father draws him' (John 6:44). No one will ask after spiritual matters unless God is at work in his life."[1]

God was at work in Ann's life. It was Ellen's turn now to be sensitive to the Holy Spirit and respond to her deeper need. She must address her quest for immediate direction in life and the more important question of where or from whom she could discover the answers. Ellen, because of her understanding of God's Word concerning spiritism and the occult, could begin to answer Ann's questions accurately and without doubt.

Not one of us knows everything the Bible teaches. The Word of God is alive, and God continually gives us new insights into the meaning of His Word as it applies to our daily lives. When we spend time in the Word, we learn more about Him. Our relationship with Him flourishes and grows in a way that understanding of His truth expands because of the development of our knowledge of Him.

God's Word is truth because He is truth. Our inability to comprehend every word does not invalidate the Bible as God's absolute standard for faith and life. In the Book of Isaiah, God tells us frankly, "'For my thoughts are not your thoughts, neither are your ways my ways,' declares the Lord. 'As the heavens are higher than the earth, so are my ways higher than your ways and my thoughts higher than your thoughts'"(Isa. 55:8–9).

The Majority May Be Wrong

Many of our friends and neighbors are searching for answers. Many voices offer solutions. In attempting to find common ground among all the people with differing views, our culture accepts every voice as valid. "Who are we to judge another or deem their voice of lesser value?" they ask. A "pluralistic society," one that embraces all views and ideas, attempts "broad-minded" acceptance of all philosophies. It neutralizes the formulation of leadership based on convictions. Few are willing to risk departure from the "norm" to stand for the singular, clearly defined truth—God's truth.

Editor Paul Ciotti wrote in the *Richmond Times-Dispatch*,

> In the name of multiculturalism we are asked not to form judgments about people who learned their values in the street . . . . Many people who grow up in the street join gangs,

deal crack cocaine, engage in drive-by shootings, have negative self-esteem, live for the moment, and place no value on human life, especially if another person has something they want, such as a ring, a watch, or an as-yet-unclaimed virginity. In the face of these kinds of values, exactly what are we supposed to do? Say this is fine; this is valid, far be it for us to discriminate against your reality that we honor and respect as much as our own?[2]

The Bible tells us that God, the Creator of the universe, and intimately involved Sustainer, alone knows what is best for us. He gives us guidelines for daily life in the Word. It is when we disregard His loving, protective instructions for our well-being and look elsewhere for direction in life that we lose our way.

Malcolm Hill, in his article "Re-establishing a Moral America," wrote, "The Bible is the only standard we have that is dependable. If we disregard it as one guide to ethics, we are left to the ocean of human views and feelings. We might as well let the 'Phil Donahue Show' be our guiding light. What do we learn from it in most cases? We learn nothing because it is full of subjectivism and has no standard by which to go."[3]

Deciding What You Believe

Return with me to Susan's story. Susan and the others whose stories I have retold are real people. I met them while traveling and speaking to women throughout the United States. Susan's dilemma is not uncommon to many women we meet every day. They may wear the latest Gucci original and project the image of success, but their hearts are torn and their spirits broken. Like Susan, they know the truth but refuse to pattern their lives by it. They suffer the inevitable consequences of choices that repudiate God's Word.

In a *McCall's* article, "Faith, Values, and Morals," it was reported, "a reader survey of faith and values has produced a complex portrait of women who derive profound strength from their spiritual beliefs but who rely on their own consciences rather than traditional church teachings to make decisions on ethical issues ranging from premarital sex and contraception to withdrawing life-support systems from terminally ill patients."[4]

Why was Susan despondent? Remember her thoughts? She had no peace within. Confusion tormented her. The words spoken privately to a friend haunted her: "I really love Steve. He's such a wonderful Christian man. We never planned to get this involved, but I believe God sent Steve to me. It's His gift. Now I know what a Christian marriage should really be like. I love Steve and can't seem to give him up."

Guilt flooded over Susan as she relived that conversation. Deep within she knew she was wrong, but Steve was meeting her needs. How could she give him up?

Deception is insidious. Satan, the author of evil, the father of lies, is the master of deception. He weaves his crooked lies to confuse, distort, and ultimately deceive and destroy. His greatest weapon is our rationalization. When we depend on our own consciences or even the traditions of the church unchecked by the Word of God, we stand precariously on the precipice of delusion. Rationalization is the easiest form of self-delusion. Through it we turn from the absolute standard of God's Word that provides an unfaltering foundation for our feet and turn to the limited insights and wisdom of human experience and knowledge.

Before making small, seemingly insignificant choices that could later lead down paths of misery and regret, remember to hold the truth of God's character and Word. By this we can make choices consistent with our love for Him and be spared the heartache of sin's inevitable consequences.

How do you do this? The following offers you simple steps for knowing what you believe.

KNOWING WHAT YOU BELIEVE

1. List the fundamental truths you know about God which apply in each situation. Search Bible references which support your basic beliefs.
2. Read these verses within the context of surrounding verses to be certain you are not "proof-texting" or taking a verse out of context to prove your point. Example: The Bible says,

"There is no God." This biblical phrase when read in the context of surrounding verses says, "The fool says in his heart, 'There is no God.'" Always read Bible verses in the context of the surrounding verses to be sure you have come to accurate conclusions.

3. List any other Bible verses which may offer further insight on the subject of concern.

4. Summarize all applicable verses in a ten-word sentence to help create a conclusive statement of belief.

5. List, read, and consider any biblical verses which might provide a different perspective or even seem contradictory to your previous conclusions.

6. Pray and ask the Holy Spirit for wisdom so that you may act with conviction on your biblical statement of belief and make choices consistent with biblical truth. Do so with compassion and mercy realizing that no one knows all the answers or holds absolute, conclusive truth but God. God's understanding far surpasses our own.

7. Thank Him for teaching you new things through His Word now and in the future, so you can say with confidence, "At this time in my spiritual life this is what I understand God's Word to mean, and I will apply it accordingly until He uses other aspects of His Word to show me differently."

8. Confidently apply God's Word in your personal life. Share His truth with others as He leads.

What truth in the Word could Susan have remembered long before this relationship captured her?

+ God never changes and His Word is truth, Isaiah 45:19.

+ God, in His protective care for His people, states, "You shall not commit adultery," Exodus 20:14.

+ God does not offer instruction arbitrarily to rob us of fun or pleasure. God knows what is best for us, Jeremiah 29:11.

+ God does all things for our good continuously conforming us into the image of His Son, Romans 8:28–29.

✦ God is all-sufficient and can be trusted to provide for the deepest needs of our hearts if we trust Him. His provision surpasses the provision any man or woman can supply, Isaiah 55:1–3; 2 Corinthians 12:9; Isaiah 54:5; Philippians 4:19.

Jesus never said that the Christian life would be easy. He simply promised He would be there to carry us through the deepest trials, offering Himself to meet our deepest needs. Susan's decision to obey God's Word, to remain faithful to her marriage vows in an unfulfilling marriage, and to break off the relationship with Steve may be the most difficult decision she will make in a lifetime, but the resultant rewards will abundantly surpass the passing pleasure to which she presently clings.

How can I be sure? Because God's Word promises that it is true. When we conform our choices to God's Word, He in turn acts in our behalf, forgiving, restoring, and honoring our obedience to Him. Our obedience is a love gift to God. It reaffirms again our love for Him above any other love in life.

Jesus tells us, "Whoever has my commands and obeys them, he is the one who loves me. He who loves me will be loved by my Father, and I too will love him and show myself to him (John 14:21). When we love God more than any other, we will express our love by desiring to do those things that please Him and bring Him joy.

Applying What You Believe

The need for moral absolutes penetrates our daily lives. What about our children? They, too, are called to be lights in a dark world. How can we prepare them to understand the trend of secular society and make informed, biblically literate decisions? Is that only possible for adults? No.

The practice of Bible-based critical decision-making can be mastered by anyone. It comes by comparing all of life to the truth of God's Word. The world cannot offer the firm foundation of God's Word. It can only offer the combined opinions of fallible men.

One mother attended an open forum at her child's school. A new value-based curriculum was being introduced. The instructor explained, "In this program, we will stress the learning of values demanded by our society and based on a common core of learning for all people. Acceptance and equal opportunity for all people and all lifestyles was the basis for a multi-cultural approach to education. Its purpose is to ensure the development of human dignity, the respect for all peoples, the understanding of differences in beliefs, values, and attitudes."

The mother felt that this denied her God-given role as a parent to teach her children the biblical values she held so dearly. What would happen to individual liberty and free choice if this system should be instituted, she thought. Suddenly it occurred to her that this new curriculum was designed to emphasize the teaching of universal values and had little to do with embracing knowledge.

What did she do? She left the room determined to take action, and she did. With a desire to help her child as well as all others, she began a community-wide campaign to educate parents about the soon-to-be-adopted curriculum. She did not use alarm tactics or abrasive methods; she simply and methodically informed every individual concerned. The curriculum didn't reach the classroom due to a unified parental accord against adopting the proposed materials.

Many renowned educators agree with both her concern and actions. Fifty years ago Mortimer Adler, chairman of the board of editors of the *Encyclopedia Britannica,* warned Americans that "our education is plagued with a departure from moral absolutes. The new terms 'common core of learning,' 'master learning,' constitute a jargon stressing self-esteem, coping skills, group goals, and preferred attitudes. It seems to genuinely threaten the values that the citizens of this country have held over the centuries."[5]

Personal choices encompass every aspect of life. When these reflect the secure absolutes of truth found in God's Word, stability is ensured. Confusion, instability, despair, and hopelessness flow from building one's life on anything other than God's Word. Even good things we cherish like church and family traditions, the wise sayings of respected persons, or the practical insights of leaders cannot supply the foundation or substitute for the security that only God's Word can provide.

Augustine, an early historian of the church, stated, "The morality of an act depends neither on its consequences or its essential nature nor its motivation but solely on whether it is in accordance with the will of God."[6]

Why? Because God alone holds the perspective of all time and eternity. He knows what He wills to accomplish in our lives and the lives of every individual. Only as we come to Him, trust Him, and follow His Word can we experience the fullness of the life He has ordained for us. "All the days ordained for me were written in your book before one of them came to be" (Ps. 139:16).

So how can we help? By evaluating our thoughts, considerations, and decisions against the truth of God's Word and by helping those with whom we are in contact, both Christian and non-Christian, to begin to search God's Word and "think biblically." We don't need to impose our thinking upon them or attempt to force them to agree with our conclusions of faith. We simply lead them to our Teacher. The Holy Spirit will teach them His truth. They need only seek Him.

Our role is to guide, leading them to the One who holds all truth: Jesus. Truly He *is* "the way, the truth, and the life." So the next time you're unsure of God's will in light of decisions you must make or actions you must take, seek God in the Word. He never contradicts His Word and His ways are always without error.

Evaluating
the Ties that Bind

Are there traditions you maintain that have no biblical basis?
Maybe you're unaware of their existence in your life,
but they hinder your ability to invest in things that matter.
How do you identify these?
Find out about the ties that needlessly bind.

"'These people honor me with their lips, but their hearts are far from me. They worship me in vain; their teachings are but rules taught by men.' You have let go of the commands of God and are holding on to the traditions of men."

MARK 7:6–8

Cynthia fumed as she hung up the telephone receiver. "Mother!" she spurted under her breath with exasperation. *She's impossible! Absolutely impossible!* Cynthia thought.

It seemed every conversation ended in an argument. It had always been that way. When would it ever change? Her mother was so irritating. She always insisted she was right and wouldn't listen to anyone else's opinion. Cynthia could hardly stand to talk to her. Now what was she to do?

Cynthia's father had died six years ago. Her mother, being so independent, took care of herself well, but now her money had run out. Cynthia was an only child and divorced. Her mother needed a place to stay. Cynthia was alone. Her mother assumed Cynthia would receive her with open arms. But Cynthia didn't feel so gracious about her mother moving in. Actually she was furious at the prospect.

She had a good income and a good life. She, too, was as independent as her mother. She didn't want to be told what to do, every decision scrutinized, every action monitored. She didn't want her mother attempting to control all aspects of her life. That's why they argued so much.

Her money was tied up elsewhere. She was investing money for the new condo she planned to buy, the one in the best part of town only moments from her office, and she had just pledged the previous Sunday to give a significant amount of money each month to the church's new building project.

If her mother were to move in that would be the end of *that* contribution. She'd already talked to Pastor Bill about her dilemma. He'd agreed that the new building was essential to God's work. He agreed if her mother could live with Aunt Edna that would solve everything. Aunt Edna was frail and had little money, yet she'd help if necessary. Why couldn't her mother live with Aunt Edna? Pastor Bill seemed to think that was a good solution. Wouldn't God rather she invest in His work at church?

Does this scenario sound familiar? It's similar to a biblical example Jesus gives when describing the convenient way we use our Christianity and tradition to absolve ourselves from responsibility consistent with biblical truth.

> And he said to them: "You have a fine way of setting aside the commands of God in order to observe your own traditions! For Moses said, 'Honor your father and your mother,' and 'Anyone who curses his father or mother must be put to death.' But you say that if a man says to his father or mother: 'Whatever help you might otherwise have received from me is Corban'(that is, a gift devoted to God), then you no longer let him do anything for his father or mother. Thus you nullify the word of God by your tradition that you have handed down. And you do many things like that."

MARK 7:9–13

Care for the elderly in a society where life span lengthens daily is an issue most of us will have to face. It is just one of many issues where the traditions of our society and even the Christian community contradict biblical truth. Nursing home facilities multiply because many grown children do not want to be bothered with the responsibility of their aging parents.

Let me introduce you to Betty Benson Robertson. Betty is an example of a woman who has taken life experiences and watched God transform the difficult and sometimes painful ones into blessings. Betty invested God's Word in her own life by making choices consistent with His Word even though the choices were difficult and unpopular.

> My father was afflicted with Parkinson's disease. He became too weak to care for himself. My mother suffered from senile

dementia. My family and I made a difficult decision. We brought my parents into our home and spent five years caring for them.

I had no idea where to run for help. My library contained only books on raising children. I often felt isolated, alone, and overwhelmed.

Then one day I watched a news report on "The Aging Game." I felt God nudging me to share with others my struggles of caring for my parents. I spent months in research and wrote the book, *Caring for Aging Parents*, published in 1992 by Beacon Hill Press.

"Honor your father and your mother"(Deut. 5:16), became the six words from Scripture that motivated my life work. Adult children are to honor their aged parents with reverence, care, and support. Sometimes it's easy to hide behind the word *impossible* when in reality, it is simply not impossible but inconvenient. I know the practical application of the scriptural mandate is a personal matter and will vary in each situation, but the directive remains.

Betty took God's Word seriously. She applied it to her own life even when it was tough. God used her obedience and blessed her with an ongoing ministry that makes an eternal difference.

Betty went on to develop a monthly newsletter, *Parent Care*, and create booklets and special reports as well as providing informative articles, useful tips, helpful suggestions, response to questions, book reviews, new product information. Inspired by God's Word, she provided guidance and encouragement to those caring for aging parents.

Her desire is that churches will "role model" the action as Jesus did! "Because we chose to care for my parents in our home instead of placing them in a nursing home, others have done the same. Our children talk freely of caring for us when we get old, if we need the care," Betty explains.

"I realize all will not bring parents into their homes, but Paul's words to Timothy, 'If anyone does not provide for his relatives, and especially for his immediate family, he has denied the faith and is worse than an unbeliever,' mean we have a responsibility to lovingly meet the needs of our aging parents to the best of our abilities."

Betty allowed God's Word to pierce her heart and transform her life. As a result He is using her to carry His "fleshed out" Word to many. What about you? Are you allowing God's Word to settle deeply in your heart, making its investment in you so that it can reach the lives of those around you?

Living "In the Word" or Traditions

How can you discover unbiblical traditions which hinder you from embracing God's Word in its purest and simplest state? These traditions fall into two categories. The first includes traditions easily recognized and evaluated by observing your own rituals and activities. These are learned through conformity to routine procedures of the Christian community or a specific denominational group. Discovering them may be simply a matter of considering why you do what you do.

The second category of traditions is not quickly apparent but is discovered after studying the Scripture and allowing God's Word to challenge why you believe what you believe. These are inwardly held traditions integrated into your belief system due to Christian teaching obtained in the past. Much Christian teaching yields fruit in a Christian's life. But some teaching may actually thwart healthy Christian growth because it is inconsistent with biblical truth.

IDENTIFYING UNBIBLICAL TRADITIONAL BELIEFS

Take this quick quiz to help you identify some traditions you may be observing that may not be based on the Bible but based instead on that lofty standard, "We've always done it this way." Put a number from 0-10 beside each statement. If you never agree with the statement put a zero. Put 1-10 to indicate your level of agreement with the statement.

1. To be a "committed" Christian you must attend a majority of the scheduled meetings of the church.
2. Those who attend the most church functions are most "spiritually minded."

3. Wearing your "Sunday best" shows your love for God and true reverence for Him.

4. You must bow your head and close your eyes when you pray for greatest effectiveness.

5. The thought of eliminating the eleven o'clock Sunday morning worship time and having "Sunday morning worship" at five in the evening makes you uncomfortable.

6. Using a more contemporary version of the Bible other than King James seems sacrilegious.

7. Missing Sunday School leaves you feeling ashamed.

8. Staying home occasionally from scheduled church services to worship God with your family or for much needed personal spiritual refreshment and rest makes you feel condemned.

9. You feel guilty if you prefer having dinner with your family at home rather than attending Wednesday night church supper.

10. You feel selfish if you don't agree to fulfill every position of responsibility asked of you in the church.

11. When you express doubts about a church leader's interpretation of a biblical passage you feel ostracized by your peers.

12. Contemporary hymns and instruments should not be used in the church worship service.

Total your score. Any number above zero shows to what degree you are maintaining traditions or beliefs that are not found in God's Word.

How can you identify these traditions and adopt a more balanced perspective in your Christian life based on God's Word rather than the traditions of men? The following questions will help you evaluate your traditions.

Personal Inventory: Clarifying Unbiblical Traditions

1. The next time you begin to fulfill any Christian observance ask yourself, Why am I doing this? Is it because someone told me I must or because the Bible teaches that God desires I fulfill this responsibility?

2. Where in the Bible do I find God's direction to do this? Look up the passage(s).

3. Read the passage(s) in context. As I read this passage, did the author intend to give a spiritual command or directive or simply to offer a word of explanation?

Example: Snake Handling—Some believe this is a command of Scripture based on Mark 16:18. Read the passage in context. Now use your *Strong's Exhaustive Concordance* to look up all other passages about snakes. Read Acts 28:3–5. God protected Paul just as He explains He will do in Mark 16. It would seem in context that Jesus is making clear that when circumstances prove dangerous as we attempt to bring the Gospel to all the tribes and nations of the world, He will protect us from harm so that His Word can be proclaimed. There is no command to handle snakes as part of a religious observance. This may seem an extreme illustration, but this is indicative of how Scripture is wrongly interpreted and how unbiblical traditions arise.

Many church traditions and outward observances have no biblical foundation. They are not necessarily wrong. These traditions cannot become a standard for evaluating Christian behavior because the Bible does not endorse them as necessary for Christian faithfulness.

God is alive. His church reflects that life only as it agrees with and adheres to the fundamentals of faith contained in God's Word. The direction the church takes in this generation will determine its effectiveness in the next decade. It is very important that our faith not degenerate into a dead list of observances devoid of meaning or vitality.

Hebrews 4:12 describes the power of the Word as "living and active. Sharper than any double-edged sword, it penetrates even to dividing soul and spirit, joints and marrow; it judges the thoughts and attitudes of the heart." This is the truth that transforms lives. We must be certain that it remains essential. All else is nonessential. As long as we do not lose ourselves by majoring in the minors, but focus on God's Word and conform to it while growing in relationship with Him, we will not stray from investing in things that matter.

The following guide will help you identify misplaced beliefs inconsistent with God's Word that may be integrated into your theology.

Identifying Misplaced Beliefs

Check the statements that apply to you.

___ When I have not kept my daily quiet time, I feel God is disappointed with me and I hesitate to talk with Him that day.

___ Sometimes I'm unsure if God likes me.

___ I don't want to worry God about the little things. He's too busy to be bothered with my concerns.

___ I'm always afraid I'm going to blow it and disappoint God.

___ I believe God helps those who help themselves.

___ I'm always comparing myself with other "committed" Christians and feel I don't measure up.

___ When all else fails I pray.

___ I believe people are basically good.

Do you know what you believe and why? The same questions offered earlier in the Personal Inventory apply. Here is an example. You believe that people are basically good.

1. When did you first come to believe this? Through the teaching in a philosophy course in college? Through a study of the Humanist Manifesto when involved in the women's lib movement of the seventies? From the book *I'm O.K. You're O.K.* in the sixties? From the teaching of a minister?
2. How can you discover a biblical perspective on this subject? Look up the word *good* in *Strong's Concordance* or the concordance in the back of your Bible. Read the passages that apply such as Matthew 19:17, "'Why do you ask me about what is good'? Jesus replied. 'There is only One who is good.'" Psalm 14:1, "The fool says in his heart, 'There is no God.' They are corrupt, their deeds are vile; there is no one who does good.'"

3. Compile the information you have received from God's Word. Ask the Holy Spirit for wisdom and truth. Consider the experiences of life. For example, the proof of original sin is found in the Bible when Adam and Eve sinned against God causing human nature to be permanently bent toward sin.

4. Reach conclusions and develop personal convictions. As you spend time with God and study His Word, He will illuminate new aspects of His character and new understanding of His Word in your life. This may alter slightly or confirm permanently your convictions, but until that time you know now what and why you be lieve. You are able to reach out to others with firm convictions and with humility, accepting that only God has all the answers and understands all things perfectly. You remain a teachable, open Christian ready to receive new insight from God at any time. In this situation, when your convictions are based on God's Word, you see that the willful pursuit of all humans to do what is not good demonstrates the truth that only God is good. When we come to faith in Jesus Christ, we enter a transformation process that allows us to exemplify the character quality of goodness but only as Christ lives out His goodness through us.

As God gives more insight on this subject, you can apply this knowledge to your accepted convictions. By evaluating them in this way, you are not creating a self-made standard and imposing it on others. You are using the standard of God's Word to touch the lives of those you meet and to provide them with vital information that will never disappoint them.

Steve Brown, author and radio commentator, did exactly this. He challenged those he met with the truth of God's Word by encouraging them to identify and evaluate their present beliefs. As pastor of a Key Buskin, Florida, church he created the "Skeptics Forum." Through newspaper advertisements he invited atheists, agnostics, and skeptics of every persuasion to an open forum to discuss biblical "contradictions" that they felt kept them from believing. Soon a weekly group was formed for further discussion with this group of "seekers." Remarkable response followed as many discovered inconsistencies in their beliefs and placed their faith in Jesus Christ.

Everett L. Wilson, in *Christianity Today*, suggested that evangelical Christians need a recognizable standard of behavior, not one based on the isolated opinions of the popular best-selling preachers or the likes and dislikes of a parent. He comments, "For example, no matter how convinced we may be in our own minds and habits, we cannot hope to insert abstinence from tobacco and alcohol into Paul's teaching concerning the body as the temple of the Holy Spirit (1 Cor. 6:18–20). As individual interpreters we may infer it from the text, but in a common understanding we may not impose it on the text."[1]

In other words, we may choose to abstain from tobacco and alcohol as a personal response to that passage, but there is nothing in the text that addresses this belief. At the same time, there are many biblical passages that encourage us to be moderate in all things, enabling us to arrive at a position of balance on this issue (Titus 1:7–8; Prov. 20:1; Eph. 5:17–18).

So we do not have the right to impose our personal choices on others. We can share our convictions hoping that they may choose to do the same as an encouragement to better health, but we do not have a biblical right to impose on others those practices that the Bible does not specifically address. If the Bible is our standard, we confine (limit) freedom as we form convictions based on truth and share them with others. When we begin to impose on others ideas that have no accurate biblical foundation, we risk heresy.

Investing your life in things that matter demands an investment of God's Word in your personal life. This enables you to identify and abandon false beliefs while maintaining and fortifying Bible-based beliefs. This frees you to accept the support that God's unchanging standard for life and growth provides.

Are these fears that keep you from risking this new adventure with God? Do they keep you from abandoning old traditions and embracing this new, Bible-based lifestyle? Learn in the next chapter how to diffuse and overcome the power of these fears.

CHAPTER FIVE

DEFUSING THE FEARS
THAT CONSTRAIN YOU

*What fears keep you from investing your life in things that matter?
Are you afraid challenges to your belief system may cause it to
crumble? Are you afraid of society's negative influence if you allow
yourself to understand its ideas? Are you afraid of the opinions of
others? How do you overcome these fears? Discover answers that
free you to invest your life in things that count.*

Perfect love drives out fear.

1 JOHN 4:18

*J*im puzzled over his dilemma. He certainly wasn't a preacher, but he simply couldn't feel comfortable with the prayer counseling "ministry" the stranger brought to the congregation. *First*, he reasoned, *I must learn more about demons. That's a topic never discussed in church.*

He pulled out his concordance and began to search every passage dealing with demons, Satan, and deliverance. It was Saturday. He had a free afternoon, so he was able to study the many passages.

Yes, demons were certainly a reality in the Bible, spoken of often by Jesus as well as others. Because Jesus is the truth He would not speak of these things just to patronize the people. Jim remembered back fifteen years ago when he was a teenager visiting an unfamiliar church. The minister said that in the time of Jesus the people attributed disease and ailment to demons. Demons weren't real, the pastor said. Jesus was simply responding to the psychology of the people.

Obviously, the minister was wrong. Jesus called illness "illness" and demons "demons," so demons must be real, Jim concluded. But the real question that perplexed Jim was the difference between demons and sin. And can Christians really be inhabited by demons as this stranger believed?

Again, Jim asked the Holy Spirit to give him direction and understanding. Through further study Jim concluded that demons were real but were messengers of Satan just as angels were messengers of God. Demons could inhabit people who opened their lives to Satan just as the Holy Spirit inhabited people who gave their lives to God. Jim saw this clearly in Luke 11:14 where Jesus drove out a demon that was mute. "When the demon left, the man who had been mute spoke, and the crowd was amazed."

Yet could demons inhabit Christians? It became clear to Jim that they could not. When the crowd said about Jesus, "By Beelzebub, the prince of demons [or Satan]," they questioned if Jesus was indeed inhabited by Satan and driving out demons by Satan's power. Jesus responded, "Any kingdom divided against itself will be ruined, and a house divided against itself will fall. If Satan is divided against himself, how can his kingdom stand?" (Luke 11:17–18)

Jim realized Jesus was saying that if Satan warred against demons who were a part of his army he would be destroying himself, an absurd pursuit.

Jim pondered this thought for a moment. He remembered Jesus' words to His disciples, "Greater is He who is in you, than He who is in the world." Jim reflected, *When a person becomes a Christian by asking Jesus Christ to be Lord of his life, the full person of God enters his or her life.* As the Hebrews declared vehemently throughout the Old Testament as foundational to their faith, "Hear, O Israel: The Lord our God, the Lord is one."

Upon belief, God indwells the believer. The person of the Holy Spirit, the very Spirit of Christ as Paul refers to Him in Acts 2:38, comes to live in the believer (John 14:26).

It became clear to Jim. "A house divided against itself cannot stand," Jesus stated clearly, so it is impossible for the Holy Spirit and the devil to dwell within the same person. The Holy Spirit is always greater and drives Satan out. "You, dear children, are from God and have overcome them, because the one who is in you [Holy Spirit] is greater than the one [Satan] who is in the world"(1 John 4:4).

Jim stood to stretch his cramped legs. He had been sitting at the kitchen table for a long time, but he knew he had his answer. Satan can oppress a believer through the manipulation of outside circumstances and situations, but he could not possess the believer or even dwell within him because the Holy Spirit would not tolerate Satan's presence. For the two to inhabit the human body together would destroy the person. God would never permit it.

Jim knew that much of what the stranger was attempting to "cast out" was actually sin that needed to be confessed and repented, not demons. Jim knew what he had to do. He'd make an appointment to speak with his pastor on Monday and share his concerns.

Fear of Examining Our Beliefs

Each of us maintains a belief system. It is comprised of interlocking beliefs obtained through personal Bible reading, listening to messages prepared by Christian leaders either from the pulpit, on the radio or television, or from conversations with family and friends. Many result from conclusions drawn from life experience. Sometimes we aren't even sure when we began to believe a certain thing or how our growing belief system developed, yet we have a vague sense that every idea hinges on others.

In the same way that a house of cards topples when one is removed, we fear that our entire faith will fall in shambles around us if one idea is challenged. Compelled by this fear, we desperately protect ourselves from these questions or the seemingly contradictory beliefs of others for fear our houses will fall and the foundations of our lives will crumble.

Jesus teaches clearly that God is not the author of fear. He is not threatened by our questions or the challenges of others. He alone is truth. His truth will stand. Considering, studying, and evaluating new ideas will either confirm the biblical truth of the beliefs we hold or aid us in developing beliefs consistent with God's Word.

No one but God can know everything. Because of our imperfection, we are constantly learning, clarifying, and substantiating the truth we hold. It is a continuing process, and in this process we are learning more about the character of God. The moment we refuse to think and consider, we refuse to grow. We in essence resign ourselves to a static existence which quickly becomes stagnant. God wants our relationship with Him to grow and flourish daily as we use all the experiences, associations, and involvements of life to learn more about Him by comparing life with the truth in His Word.

Creating a biblically-based "belief grid" equips us to make decisions based on God's truth. We use the "whole counsel of God" as our standard for developing this grid rather than proof-texting and always remain prepared to hone the elements of this grid for precision and accuracy.

Thus, we welcome the sharpening of the "belief grid" by evaluating challenging ideas and fresh insights. And we never need to fear because God never changes. His Word never changes. He and His Word can be trusted. Nothing new we ever learn about God will alter that.

Fear of What We Can't Explain and Don't Understand

Tom Peters, in his article "The New Builders," wrote,

> Information technology is driving most of today's and tomorrow's change. If one doesn't understand it, have a very good feel for it, he or she will not be able to create and then exploit the emerging opportunities (either in firm structure, inter-firm structure, or product/service development).
>
> If we desire to have an impact in our society, technology is proving to be one of the most effective ways we can do so. Yet the Christian community seems to exemplify an almost irrational fear concerning these new discoveries God is initiating on our world today. Preachers use modern technological discoveries as "End Time" indicators.[1]

Has that been your perspective? Do you condemn that which you don't understand with religious jargon because of your fear of the unknown? Well, you're not alone. Christians have been doing this throughout the ages.

Copernicus and Galileo exemplify those caught between truth revealed through God's creation and the obstinate fears of the church. Let me share their stories with you.

In 1543 Copernicus risked the church's wrath to publish a mathematical description of the solar system titled, "The Revolution of the Heavenly Orbs." In it he described the solar system as a single system revolving around the sun. His suggestion that the sun was the center of planetary orbit rather than the earth sparked outrage from the Roman Catholic Church.

The Catholic Church was so committed to the belief that the heavens circled the earth, the belief became a tenant of the faith as if ordained by God Himself. Copernicus died the year his book was published, but Galileo built upon his discoveries. Galileo, scientist and mathematician, soon followed in Copernicus' footsteps by inventing the most high-powered telescope of his day. In his book, *The Starry Messenger*, issued during the period September 1609 to March 1610, Galileo describes his discoveries.

(I have seen) stars in myriads, which have never been seen before, and which surpass the old, previously known stars in number more than ten times.

But that which will excite the greatest astonishment by far, and which indeed especially moved me to call the attention of all astronomers and philosophers, is this, namely, that I have discovered four planets, neither known nor observed by any astronomers before my time.[2]

Can you imagine Galileo's exuberant wonder at these new discoveries? Yet Galileo was denounced, ostracized, interrogated, humiliated, and threatened with torture by the "church" of his era. He was forced to write the following at the age of seventy, after a trial over which the Pope presided.

I Galileo Galilei, . . . after an injunction had been judicially intimated to me by this Holy office, to the effect that I must altogether abandon the false opinion that the sun is the centre of the world, and moves, and that I must not hold, defend, or teach it in any way whatsoever, verbally or in writing, the said doctrine, and after it had been notified to me that the said doctrine was contrary to Holy Scripture—I wrote and printed a book in which I discuss this doctrine already condemned, and adduce arguments of great cogency in its favour, without presenting a solution of these; and for this cause I have been pronounced by the Holy Office to be vehemently suspected of heresy, that is to say, of having held and believed that the sun is the centre of the world and immovable, and that the earth is not the center and moves:

Therefore desiring to remove from the minds of your Eminances, and of all faithful Christians, this strong suspicion, reasonably conceived against me, with sincere heart and unfeigned faith I abjure, curse, and detest the aforesaid errors and heresies.[3]

Galileo was forced to deny the truth because it contradicted the unbiblical traditions of the church. God is the God of all truth. No discovery will ever be made that God has not first allowed. No discovery of science or technology will ever contradict the Christian faith because it is based on the very person and writing of the one who is truth Himself.

Jesus Christ says clearly, "I am the way, the truth, and the life"(John 14:6). In response to Job's questioning, God's words reverberate throughout the ages, "Where were you when I laid the earth's foundation? Tell me, if you understand. Who marked off its dimensions? Surely you know!" (Job 38:4–5, continue reading through verse 39). The God of all time and eternity is in control of all His creation, and He alone determines the boundaries of man's discovery. Nothing escapes His notice or defies His command.

So why do we fear? Charles E. Hummel, in his *Christianity Today* article "Making Friends With Galileo" wrote, "First, contrary to long-standing mythology, his (Galileo's) science and theology were not enemies but partners—two 'books of God'. God is known by Nature in his words, and by doctrine in His revealed Word."[4]

At one time, technological advances alarmed the church as well. Advancing technology and the resultant globalization, the ability to communicate with the world as easily as with your neighbor through the "information highway," attracted negative press in the Christian media, who decried globalization as a "world system" indicative of the "end times."

These are the "end times." Every day since Jesus died and rose from the dead moves us nearer to the time when He will come again in glory. We often forget that when Jesus said, "No one knows about that day or hour, not even the angels in heaven, nor the Son, but only the Father" (Matt. 24:36). The Greek word *chronos* means "chronology." No one can know the chronology of these events and at best can only speculate on the significance of particular discoveries. So what is at the root of our fears?

Is it a fear of the unknown, something you don't understand? Or is it linked to some teaching you have heard that attributes evil to inanimate objects incapable of decision-making? As with all discoveries the hands that initiate and operate them are the determining factor. So why should Christian hands be still? Should Christians stop pursuing discovery? Should we stop exploring and learning because the enemy has deceived us into fear and withdrawal?

The fields of technology, medicine, and science are harmless in themselves. God is NOT the author of fear, and His "perfect love drives out fear" (1 John 4:18). Why not evaluate the data of new discoveries? Compare them to the truth of God's Word. You may disagree with the assumptions, assertions, or conclusions science, technology, and medicine infer but you need not fear. Nothing will prove God false or His Word untrue.

Look at the testimonies of Jack Lousma, member aboard *Skylab 3* and the space shuttle *Columbia*, and James Irwin, one who experienced one of the greatest technological feats of the twentieth century, walking on the moon. Jack explains that his experiences on *Skylab 3* "reinforced my faith that there was a God who created the world. From what I've seen up there, it is clear that a Master Creator and Planner made it (the world) happen."[5]

James Irwin exclaims, "The hours spent on the moon were the most thrilling of my life, not because I was there, but because I could feel the Presence of God. There were times when I was faced with new challenges, and help from God was immediate."[6]

Fear of What Others Think

Jenny wavered when Mike motioned for her to leave the choir loft and join the family during the Sunday service. Mike didn't know Christ. Jenny prayed for years that Mike's interest in spiritual things would heighten. Lately he decided to join the family during Sunday services. Jenny was delighted, seeing this as God's answer to her prayers. But Mike didn't feel comfortable. He didn't like the fact that Jenny sang in the choir and sat apart from him. Jenny didn't know how to explain that getting up after the anthem in the middle of the service and joining him was not allowed. She was sure it was considered unacceptable even though no one had mentioned it.

Mike motioned again. What was Jenny to do? Getting up in front of her peers would be embarrassing, maybe even humiliating if her movement attracted attention and caused a distraction to the congregation.

She prayed silently, *Lord, what do I do? I have to join Mike. He wouldn't understand otherwise. For so long I have tried to fulfill Your word:* "Be submissive to your husbands so that, if any of them do not believe the word, they may be won over without words by the behavior of their wives, when they see the purity and reverence of your lives"(1 Pet. 3:1–2). *Mike wouldn't be angry if I stayed here, simply hurt.*

She continued, *You know I love to sing in the choir. It's Your gift that I return to You for Your glory. I don't think You want me to quit. Lord, is there any Bible verse that directly commands that a choir member must stay in the choir loft for the entire service?*

Jenny smiled at the thought that God would write such a thing. Of course not. Without another thought, Jenny quietly stood and inched her way out of the loft. She walked through a hallway behind the church sanctuary, reentered from the rear of the sanctuary, and joined Mike.

Have you ever felt like Jenny? You fear the opinions of others more than you fear God Himself. Because of rigid rules and routines in the church, you hesitate to do anything that might challenge the status quo. God wants to deliver you from these fears. They are both ungodly and unbiblical.

His desire is that you live according to His Word as directed by the Holy Spirit. When we come to Christ, we experience the freeing joy of knowing His love, the love that is unconditional, not deserved and cannot be earned. We walk in this freedom as we walk with Him.

Through Paul's words to the Galatians, God speaks clearly to this problem. "Am I now trying to win the approval of men, or of God? Or am I trying to please men? If I were still trying to please men, I would not be a servant of Christ" (Gal. 1:10). Has your desire to keep a set of rules and regulations for men replaced your desire to please God by sharing a relationship with Him, trusting Him to show you what to do according to His Word and the guidance of His Holy Spirit?

That's what the Galatians did. We read of Paul's exasperation with them.

> You foolish Galatians! Who has bewitched you? Before your very eyes Jesus Christ was clearly portrayed as crucified. I would like to learn just one thing from you: Did you receive the Spirit by observing the law, or by believing what you heard? Are you so foolish? After beginning with the Spirit, are you now trying to attain your goal by human effort? Have you suffered so much for nothing—if it really was for nothing? Does God give you his Spirit and work miracles among you because you observe the law, or because you believe what you heard?

GALATIANS 3:1–5

As you desire to invest your life in things that matter, it is important to determine what matters to God. Many of the rituals and behaviors we conform to as a desire to please our peers don't matter to God at all. When you're unsure of what God would have you do in a situation or your desire is to determine what matters to God, ask yourself the following questions:

THE DESIRES OF GOD
VS. THE OPINIONS OF MEN

1. What is my dilemma?
2. Pray and ask the Holy Spirit to help you answer the question, "What does the Bible say in reference to this issue?"
3. If you are unsure of any specific reference to your issue in the Bible ask yourself, "Does what I want to do, say, or think directly contradict my knowledge of God's character?" God will never lead you to do anything that contradicts His Word or character.

4. Follow the Holy Spirit's leading as He reveals God's will for you.

God wants us to be free from the fears that constrain us. He wants us to walk in confidence directed by His Word and Spirit. Fear is a powerful tool used by Satan and sometimes others to dominate us and control our thoughts and behavior. Often fear of rejection by the Christian community, similar to that of "shaming" used by the Quakers in the past, inhibits us from adopting and applying biblical truth in the secular world. Fear of the secular world and its impact on our lives, which some Christian leaders promote, obstructs our ability to invest our lives in things that matter. Identifying and defusing the personal fears that hinder us may be the greatest step we make concerning a life investment that produces eternal dividends for God.

Take time now to evaluate the fears that hinder or possibly paralyze you in risking the investment of your life for God. Give these fears to Him. He'll deliver you. He will answer your prayer. He came to set the captive free. That includes you and me.

PART TWO

It's More

Than the Thought

that Counts

*N*ow that you're on the road to an ongoing lifestyle of sharp biblical thinking, it's necessary to consider the integration of these biblical values in a way that will alter attitudes and actions. Your attitudes are the clothing your thinking wears. Your actions are the "fashion show" of the clothing. Both negative and positive affect your life investment.

This section focuses on translating sharp, biblical thinking into biblically consistent attitudes and behavior. I've often said to Christian groups, if you find joy in the Christian life you need to let your face know. Attitudes portray your thoughts' emotions, and actions demonstrate your attitudes. If you see a hungry person on the street you may think, *I would like to help that person.* If you offer help with a haughty or condescending attitude, your action communicates something quite different."

So, as you continue in your life investment strategy, it is important to consider the attitudes and actions you communicate. Are they consistent with the message you bear?

———————

CHAPTER SIX

Defeating the Dragon Within

*Have personal insecurities caused you to reflect critical or
judgmental attitudes toward others? How can you defeat the
dragon within? Or are the insecurities of others making you a
scapegoat for their cruel and malicious words? How can you face
the animosity of others with confidence in God's Word and will?*

For He has set a day when he will judge the world with justice by the man he has appointed.

ACTS 17:31

You really ought to be home more. You can't do that and work," June blurted to the younger pastor's wife. "Pastors' wives shouldn't be working anyway. It's a bad witness to those in the community. How can the pastor do his job and help with the children while you're working?"

Mary's heart felt like a boulder sinking to the bottom of the sea. Oh, no. Not again. June can't give it up. June sat in her expensive Cadillac, the epitome of wealth and leisure. At age seventy she probably had never had a financially needy day in her life. Mary's mind wandered while June droned on. She heard phrases through the maze of her own preoccupation. "*My* daughter-in-law quit her job to stay home with her children. Her husband insisted on it. Women should be in the home. You should be doing what Titus 2 says. You should be 'busy at home.'"

Mary's mind reviewed the last seventeen years of her life as a pastor's wife and mother. While her children were small, she had done exactly that. She'd stayed at home trying to create every small business opportunity there was to augment her husband's sparse salary. Nine thousand dollars a year wasn't very much even in those days. She had sewn and tailored for neighbors, embroidered counted cross-stitch pictures to sell, cooked, cleaned, done anything she could think of to make extra income while staying at home.

She remembered the years when the refrigerator was bare and a pot of vegetable soup had to stretch for a week. She cringed at the humiliation of going to church in a day smock from the department store lingerie department because she couldn't afford a maternity dress before the first child was born.

June didn't have those memories. She didn't know how deeply and painfully her judgmental attitudes cut Mary. When all the children were in school, Mary had begun to look for part-time work to help out with the bills. She created a part-time business at home, attempting to do her job while still being there for the children when they returned from school. As the children grew, bills grew as well. To stay out of debt, more money was needed. So she moved outside the home in search for work.

Mary didn't want to work outside the home. But there were so many bills. Mary sought work in the hopes of lifting the depression that clouded her husband's life.

No, June didn't understand, and there was no way to explain it to her because her mind was closed. In the past whenever Mary attempted to respond to June's comments of condemnation and criticism, June simply went on about her daughter-in-law, who was such a good mother, and the bad witness of working mothers.

The truth was June couldn't afford to be wrong. Any weak link in her theology might mean that some or all of what she believed was false, and that was intolerable. Her security as a person rested in her rightness. The sad thing was that her rigid rightness hurt so many around her. It was more important for June to be right than to care for those she so constantly judged.

Understanding the Dragon in the Word

Mary is not alone. All of us at times have felt threatened when others challenged our point of view or questioned our "rightness" about something. Fear and insecurity are gripping emotions. We do everything we can to keep them at bay. To overcome their assault we build rigid belief systems that must go unchallenged. When we are challenged, our comfortable patterns of thinking and living are assaulted. We either retaliate or withdraw into self-righteous indignation.

When our security is in anything but God, we live in constant threat of disillusionment and disappointment. Jesus addressed this issue, "You diligently study the Scriptures because you think that by them you possess eternal life. These are the Scriptures that testify about me, yet you refuse to come to me to have life" (John 5:39–40). Even when we use the Bible to construct legalistic lists of "dos" and "don'ts" to live by and impose on others, we have failed to place our trust in the One who is its source. The Bible is God's autobiography. He desires that we see His face through every word, come to know Him more intimately, and find our security in Him.

Ted Ward, in his book, *Values Begin at Home*, wrote,

> Consider the difference between rules and principles. Rules are external. They are the voices of others—of society, of my nation, of God. But principles are internal. I can't bring rules in because they belong to the outside; but I *can* bring principles in. Principles are what I have selected and brought in from what I respect and value.
>
> If God's Law means rules and regulations, it is outside of me. But if God's Law means principles, it can come inside and transform me. God wants His people to be changed on the *inside*. God prefers that His Law be written inside on the heart rather than just inscribed on tablets of stone (2 Cor. 3:3).[1]

We must internalize God's truth in a way that changes us on the inside. We must invest God's Word in our personal lives before we can invest it in the lives of others, which means we must not put a mental lock on our minds, disallowing new ideas or fresh insights God desires to give us. What "pet doctrines" are incorporated in your belief system that, when threatened, cause you to treat others in a condemning or judgmental way?

PERSONAL JUDGMENT SURVEY

Place the number 0 beside those statements that do not reflect your beliefs and 1–10 beside those that most reflect your beliefs.

1. Working moms are not obedient to God and His Word.
2. Home school moms are more spiritual.
3. Elderly members of the congregation are out of touch with the world and aren't interested in the ministry of the church.

4. If a man plays golf on Sunday morning, he doesn't have a heart for God.
5. Women's ministry activities in the church are for women who don't have anything better to do.
6. Those who help in the nursery or with church kitchen responsibilities are the ones who *really* have a "servant's heart."
7. A Christian who doesn't carry his Bible to church isn't as committed to God as one who does.
8. A Christian couldn't possibly smoke a cigarette, drink wine with dinner, or dance at a wedding.
9. Homeless people are only homeless because they are poor money managers.
10. Teenagers who wear jeans to church are rebellious.

Every one of these statements is a value judgement. They do not take into account the circumstances, needs, concerns, or situations of the people involved. Did responding to these statements stir some discomfort?

You may ask, Doesn't 1 Corinthians 14 give us a responsibility to judge? "But if an unbeliever or someone who does not understand comes in . . . he will be convinced by all that he is a sinner and will be judged by all" (1 Cor. 14:24). Judging in this context refers to identifying the authenticity of someone's faith. Why? So that we will not be deceived by following someone who is an unbeliever or is deceived himself. Discerning truth to protect ourselves from deception is very different than judging for the purpose of condemnation or shunning.

As we invest our lives in God's Word, He will help us remove judgments and criticism that hinder us from reaching out to others. We can invest and share God's Word with compassion and genuine concern. We do it not to prove we are right or for the sake of our own pride or self-image. We do it because we love God first and desire to extend that love and abundant joy of life with Him to all we meet.

Jesus explained this succinctly to a Pharisee when He said, "'Love the Lord your God with all your heart and with all your soul and with all your mind.' This is the first and greatest commandment. And the second is like it: 'Love your neighbor as yourself.' All the Law and the Prophets hang on these two commandments" (Matt. 22:37–40). Jesus explains that the heart and soul of God's values can be found in relationships—a relationship first with Him and then with those He has placed in our lives. All the value directives in the Scripture hinge on and are included in these two principles.

When our lives do not reflect these values and our belief systems are challenged, we perceive this as a threat. Due to our insecurities, we console ourselves with critical and judgmental attitudes.

For example, without even realizing her thought patterns, June may be thinking, *It threatens my belief system that this mother works, manages her home, and loves her husband and children. I see that her children love God and their parents. Rather than being forced to reevaluate what I believe, I'll condemn, judge, and criticize this woman.*

Then if her criticisms do not affect Mary's behavior and force her to stop working, June shares her "concerns" about this working mother with others, soliciting support for her position. She thinks agreement will prove her point.

This sad commentary is too often a reality in the Christian community. Unfortunately, everyone suffers. Women like Mary are attacked. June and those who agree with her judgements live with the misery of their own resentment, bitterness, and hostility at Mary's unwillingness to conform. They reap the consequences of participating in vicious gossip. The church, the body of Jesus Christ, is divided. And worst of all, the name of Jesus is maligned before the watching secular world.

Defeating the Dragon

To invest our lives in things that matter we must be delivered from attitudes of criticism and condemnation and take on the character of Christ. Even when people did not do as Jesus desired, He responded with compassion.

Jesus spoke lovingly, "O Jerusalem, Jerusalem, you who kill the prophets and stone those sent to you, how often I have longed to gather your children together, as a hen gathers her chicks under her wings, but you were not willing" (Matt. 23:37). He longed to see the very people who had rejected and attacked Him come near to experience His love.

Recently I read an article written by an influential, sensitive teacher who related experiences where God used her mightily in reaching the hearts as well as minds of several students in the public school system. I was grieved as I read her final statements though. She closed her article with a statement no one in the Christian community has the freedom to overlook.

"If I regret anything about teaching, it's the fact that I've been criticized for being a working mother. (That's always surprised me because when I was in Brazil and did the same thing as a missionary, I was praised.) What if all the mothers who teach pulled out? What would our country be?"[2]

Does this mean we compromise the truth of Scripture? Absolutely not. It means that we internalize God's truth, desiring to be transformed in a way that we exemplify God's character and then invest in things that matter by listening, understanding, caring, and then sharing His truth. Our responsibility is to share the truth of God as we understand it, then leave the rest up to God while we consistently exemplify the character of God's love and compassion to others. We are not God. He is working in the lives of all Christians, and He will show them the application of His truth in their lives if they are listening, open, and willing.

What if you know people who aren't open or don't conform to His truth as you view it? Their choices ultimately are between God and themselves. They are accountable to Him. Their bad choices will reap the inevitable repercussions of sin. If you have lovingly spoken the truth, your responsibility has ended. Your only remaining responsibility is to continue loving them in Jesus. You can impose God's truth on no one.

Jesus left us this example. "As for the person who hears my words but does not keep them, I do not judge him. For I did not come to judge the world, but to save it" (John 12:47). Our role is to live as Jesus did, always with a desire for restoration and reconciliation. Rejecting personal prejudices and following God's perspective of caring frees us to move unhindered out of our comfort zones into the world.

CHAPTER SEVEN

How You Feel
about What You Think

Does your biblical thinking translate into biblical values?
What are biblical values and how do you apply them?
Do you have difficulty making choices
consistent with these values for fear of estranging family
and friends who may not agree?
Making choices consistent with your values is possible.

He said to them, "You are the ones who justify yourselves in the eyes of men, but God knows your hearts. What is highly valued among men is detestable in God's sight."

LUKE 16:15

*K*en stared with unbelief at the teenager across from him. Masking his astonishment, he struggled to form an appropriate response. He knew tutoring kids from the local high school wasn't going to be easy, but the things they said never ceased to amaze him.

"I don't know how to write my name," Jeff announced. "I'm sixteen and I can't read or write. My dad is big in Amway, and he has enough money to keep me in fancy clothes and cars for life. I don't need a job, and I don't need an education to get a job. I just want to learn to write so I can sign my name. They said you could help. Will you help me? Don't tell my dad I'm here. He says I don't need to learn nothin.' He'd be mad at me for coming."

Tom Ray, like Ken, meets weekly with kids who come to be tutored with problems even he can't imagine. "I'm just a country boy," remarks Tom in response to questions about his numerous academic qualifications. His rich, Southern drawl and lopsided grin purposely mock any hint of professional polish. An employee at one of the largest, most successful chemical companies in the world, Tom has a degree in mechanical engineering, with expertise in mechanical, electrical, chemical, and civil engineering.

Tom Ray tutors kids in the high school because he can see the shift away from values in today's kids. He wants to help. "You know," Tom remarks, "God has used a lot more things in my life than a degree and engineer's license. Actually, I tutor kids who need help at the high school because God has used this as a terrific opportunity to question the kids about their values. It has been an eye opener. Many of them are not only off track, they don't even know where the track is. I pray that God will use me to help them evaluate their values and establish priorities at this critical time in their lives."

Why? Because values reflect attitudes which in turn clothe beliefs. The young man we met at the beginning of this chapter is being reared by a dad who thinks money is "life." Greed drives him. As long as his son has money, he has it all. Greed permeates our society. Greed is a value, an unbiblical value, but still a value.

In a recent *PARADE* magazine article in answer to the question, "What should mankind aim to accomplish in the coming decade?" playwright August Wilson wrote, "We should make greed the sin of all sins, so that greedy people all over the planet are shunned. It is greed that leads to thievery, lying, cheating, and stealing, which leads to wars, which leads to murders, which leads to all sorts of other things. Unless we succeed, I don't know that we are going to see the 22nd century."[1]

Interesting commentary on our culture and values from a secular writer. What do you value? Do you know? Have your biblical beliefs been translated into attitudes and values that you can in turn invest in your own world?

Family Values—What Are They?

"Family values" became the buzzword of the nineties. But what are family values? Are they traditions held because of cultural attitude, or are they values maintained because of biblical consistency? Are we basing our Christian values on the experiences of past generations or biblical truth? Judith Timson offers an interesting view on family values for every Christian to consider in her article, "Family Values—Not!!!"

> There is no doubt we all have a deep unease about our complex lives, a desire for a safer haven. But there is no safe haven and there never was . . . So, what were they all harking back to? Was it to the fifties when men were imprisoned in their grey-flannel straitjackets, working so much they were barely home, while women were advised by their doctors that a little antidepressant might be in order for that "blue" feeling they experienced as they watched their lives being defined by kitchen walls

and the needs of others? . . . Or maybe it was the value of women being seen and not heard?

That phrase, "family values" is as loaded with false sentimentality as apple pie and motherhood, and as empty of real meaning."[2]

Then what are family values? Who will provide the appropriate definition? This is as crucial a question as it is fundamental. As you walk daily with God and resolutely choose to align your thinking with God's Word, you may be the person God wills to establish and communicate His values to a waiting world.

What does value mean? Webster's dictionary defines it as "that quality of a thing which is thought to be more or less desirable, useful, estimable, important, etc.; worth or degree of worth . . . that which is desirable or worthy of esteem for its sake; thing or quality having intrinsic worth." Christians should value above all else our relationship with God. How do we communicate this to others? We allow our attitudes and actions to communicate His truth.

What are the practical implications of that communication? You must decide what you value. I'll never forget Marvin Wilson, professor of Old Testament at Gordon College, declaring passionately, "Don't fight about anything that's not worth dying for." What is of that great value to you? How can you discover the answer to that question? Try the following personal survey.

Identifying Your Values

1. Pray, and then list ten biblical values you most greatly prize. (If you knew you were to die tomorrow, what ten values would you want to list and leave with your children?) You may want to compile a draft copy and prayerfully think about this for several days or weeks.

2. Beside each item on your value list, write biblical references that support each value. Do you believe these things solely because you were taught to value them or because God's Word gives foundation for such values?

3. How do you presently communicate these values to others in your life? Consider this question carefully. Describe specific events when you communicated each of these values to another person.

4. Do your attitudes and actions reflect your own beliefs accurately, or are you perceived as simply imposing accepted values on another? Without compromising your values, how can you improve your communication so you are more easily understood by those you desire to influence?

Dennis Hensley, professor of English at Ball State University, expressed his concern. "It worries me greatly that the younger generations are not instilled with a basic understanding of core values, such as respect for authority (teachers, police, government officials), respect for the elderly, respect for people's property, respect for female virtues, respect of marital obligations, and respect for one's country." Dennis knows that he can't cure all the ills of the world. "Even so," he says, "as such, I decided to invest myself in ways that I can do the most good in my areas of strength."

Dennis has served as chairman of the school board of a private Christian elementary school for eleven years. "I use my talent to help develop a curriculum that will produce well-educated, God-honoring, well-mannered young people.

"In this 'me first' world, no one shows respect for anyone else. This leads to chaos, such as gang violence, street riots, increased robberies and the random shooting we are seeing so much of these days. I have raised my two children to know that their rights do not extend to a point of anyone else's inconvenience or ill-treatment.

"I feel that if each person would take one or two areas of special interest and focus intently on improving this area, we'd see great changes worldwide."

LaDonne James recognizes the value struggle Tom Ray and Dennis Hensley speak of in her neighborhood and profession. "I work with children, and I see that lack of values affects every area of their young lives. Some of my students do not come from Christian homes. They are 'unchurched' and literally do not know that stealing, cursing, immorality, etc., are not acceptable standards. They witness this behavior on every hand and consider it the norm. It is the first time they have been told about morals, ethics, and about God's standards for our lives."

Defining and clothing your biblical thinking with attitudes and actions consistent with your beliefs matters. What greater privilege than to know that you are investing God's Word in the lives of others for the sake of Jesus? To know that the dividends count for eternity?

Your biblical values can have profound effects on a culture drowning in the sea of situational ethics, neutralism, subjectivism, relativism, and many other "isms." Many of your friends, neighbors, and loved ones have been denied the security of a single standard for determining ethical attitudes and behavior. They carry the crushing burden of creating their own standard for right and wrong, good and evil, a standard doomed to fail and certain to lead them to destruction.

In an attempt to embrace all values and standards of behavior as worthy, our world flounders, hopelessly looking for direction and assurance—an assurance that its choices have merit and hope for a better future. Yet the hope is a mirage. There is no oasis of peace and security.

Finding the Source of Values in the Word

Paul protects us from trusting this mirage when he said, "Therefore, I urge you, brothers, in view of God's mercy, to offer your bodies as living sacrifices, holy and pleasing to God—this is your spiritual act of worship. Do not conform any longer to the pattern of this world, but be transformed by the renewing of your mind. Then you will be able to test and approve what God's will is—his good, pleasing and perfect will" (Rom. 12:1–2).

How can you form values that more accurately represent God's character and truth? By spending time reading and discussing His

Word with Him. As your thinking changes, your values, attitudes, responses, and actions will follow. Rather than allowing the world's value system to "squeeze you into its mold" (Rom. 12:2) as the Phillips translation describes, God's Word shapes your thoughts and, in turn, your values. With the Holy Spirit's power you will be able to observe and evaluate the personal motivations and impulses that drive you, helping you recognize whether they reflect an accurate or inaccurate understanding of God's Word.

Sharing God's Values with the World

Materialism, greed, selfishness, and disrespect for authority are a few of the values our society promotes. You can make a difference. If you allow your life to adopt thinking consistent with God's Word, your values will be transformed. Your life will produce the fruit Jesus speaks of. "I am the [true] vine; you are the branches. If a man remains in me and I in him, he will bear much fruit; apart from me you can do nothing. . . .This is to my Father's glory, that you bear much fruit, showing yourselves to be my disciples. . . . You did not choose me, but I chose you and appointed you to go and bear fruit—fruit that will last" (John 15:5, 8, 16).

Your life becomes a testimony to all you meet as you make choices consistent with your biblical value system. This proved to be true for Alvin and Dorothy Kauffman. Before marriage, Alvin and Dorothy decided they wanted more than a nice house, two cars and a two-week vacation every year. So, three years ago, they left their home in Detroit with their one-year-old son, Lee, to "step out into the water." They moved to China.

They loved the Chinese people. "As a teacher," Dorothy said, "I had instant credibility. They called me a 'foreign expert.' They trusted me. My students showed great respect. That gave me a myriad of opportunities to share my life, my expertise, and my Christian love in and outside the classroom. That's when our students became our friends."[3]

No matter where you live, as you "flesh out" the truth of God's Word by the power of the Holy Spirit, lives will be touched and you will be investing your life in more than the passing of finite moments and days. You will be investing your life in things that last. Learn in the next chapter about the way God has uniquely equipped you for your investment.

———————

VALUING THE PERSON CHRIST HAS MADE YOU

Do you have difficulty deciding God's purpose for your life?
Is it your desire to identify and use your God-given gifts, talents,
and abilities?
Valuing the unique person you continue to become in Christ
enables you to develop and use the gifts He gives for His glory,
honor, and praise.

We have different gifts, according to the grace given us.
ROMANS 12:6

*T*ara huddled in the corner of her overstuffed couch. Tears, black with mascara, dripped from her chin. Her husband and two children left long ago. The house was quiet and empty—terribly empty. Now there was time to grieve.

Grief was good. She had needed it. Her pent up emotions needed a release. Life had not turned out the way she imagined. Unrealized expectations and dark disillusionment clouded her thinking. The mirage of "happily ever after" died years ago after her choices robbed her of husband and children. She rehearsed the memories carefully, grieving their reality, so that she could finally go on with her life. It was time.

Tom, her husband, had discovered her unfaithfulness one evening when he came home from work on time. He hadn't done that in years. Working overtime was his way of life. He left at 7:00 A.M., and she wouldn't see him again until he slipped under the covers at midnight or later. She managed everything alone, and that was the pattern.

Only months before, Tara met Jim. It happened one day quite by accident. She literally bumped into him turning the corner of the grocery store cereal aisle. They both apologized profusely and laughed as they reached for the same cereal. Feeling awkward and saying little more, they moved on.

In the weeks that followed they passed on the street, picked children up at the same preschool, and met often in the grocery store. Finally he suggested they have coffee at the neighborhood coffee shop. From that point they both found a companionship and relationship that replaced their loneliness. He was divorced and she abandoned, in a manner of speaking.

On that particular day, Tom returned home unannounced. She never knew why. On that same, fateful day, Tara had finally agreed to put the children to bed early and spend the evening with Jim.

Tom was early, terrified to find her gone. He called the police and every imaginable neighbor, friend, and relative. She returned home at midnight only to discover the flashing lights of police cars that circled her house. She rushed in, afraid something had happened to the children. Her misdeed was discovered.

She tried to lie, but there had been other times Tom had been unable to reach her by phone. As a result his suspicions were aroused.

The thought that she had left her babies alone to meet another man shocked her. She couldn't believe it herself, but it had happened and she paid for it dearly. Divorce followed. Judged an unfit mother, Tara lost custody of her children. The memories pierced her soul. They flooded over her as she tasted every aspect of the grief. Jim quickly disappeared from her life, and she was left alone.

Things were different for her now. One Wednesday night, while traveling through Texas to her mother's home in Mississippi, her despair overwhelmed her. Seeing the church lights, she wandered into a small mission church and took a seat in the back. For the first time in her life she heard of a love greater than any she had known—a forgiving love that was extended to anyone no matter how horrible his or her mistake. An eternal love.

She had never been in church before. She remembered praying with the speaker to receive this love that was available only through faith in God's Son, Jesus Christ. She remembered the love the church people shared after the program. She was amazed at the light shining in their eyes, the glow their faces seemed to radiate.

Now, years later, Tara allowed herself to grieve. God's goodness had kept her. Though Tom had long since remarried, and his new wife had adopted the children, God had blessed her by allowing her to touch the lives of other children. She now taught in the local elementary school and directed the church choir. God's Word permeated her life, and He was using her daily to affect the lives of other children when she couldn't reach her own.

Now it was time to forgive herself. While she grieved over broken dreams, she realized God is the God of dreams. He alone can create something out of nothing. Loving her, He forgave her and redesigned the broken dreams of her life into a magnificent, stained-glass portrait—a portrait radiantly glimmering in the noonday sun. He redeemed the rubble, perfected her gifts and talents, and used her for His greater glory. She was making differences that counted for eternity.

God's Redeeming Power in You

I met Tara in that little Texas church the night she came to meet Jesus. When she visited us later, we saw her transformed. Her attitudes had changed. We watched a deeply hurt, hardened, angry, and disillusioned young woman become lovely, transformed by God's loving tenderness. Her gratitude to God never diminished. She grew to value herself as she recognized the intensity with which God valued her. She allowed God to develop her gifts and talents in a way so that He could use her to touch many others.

And you? What is your story? Every Christian has one, you know. Do you know the love of God in a way that is daily transforming your life? Have you yielded yourself to Him so that the gifts, skills, and talents He has given you flourish as His Word transforms your thoughts and attitudes?

As our thinking and attitudes reflect a biblically accurate representation of God and His Word, we grow to respect ourselves as valued and gifted by God. Psalm 139 becomes a reality in our lives.

> O LORD, you have searched me and you know me. . . .
>   you are familiar with all my ways. . . .
> You hem me in—behind and before;
>   you have laid your hand upon me.
> Such knowledge is too wonderful for me, . . .
> even there your hand will guide me,
>   your right hand will hold me fast. . . .
> even the darkness will not be dark to you;
>   the night will shine like the day,
>   for darkness is as light to you.

For you created my inmost being;
>you knit me together in my mother's womb.
I praise you because I am fearfully and wonderfully made;
>your works are wonderful, . . .
My frame was not hidden from you
>when I was made in the secret place.
When I was woven together in the depths of the earth,
>your eyes saw my unformed body.
All the days ordained for me,
>were written in your book
>before one of them came to be.
How precious to me are your thoughts, O God!
>How vast is the sum of them!

PSALM 139: 1,3, 5–6, 10, 12–17

God's Security

There is great security in knowing that God's all-encompassing love and care never change. Nothing escapes His notice. He knows us exactly as we are. Fully aware of both our shortcomings and strengths, He loves us. And as an outgrowth of that love, He develops the gifts, talents, and abilities He has given us as a testimony to His love. There is great assurance in the promise that "God's gifts and his call are irrevocable" (Rom. 11:29). When we trust Him, He allows us to participate with Him in His purposes for time and eternity. This remarkable privilege is ours—the opportunity to invest our lives in things that matter for eternity.

This comes by first yielding to Him. His Holy Spirit gives us the power to do His will as we allow Him to work in our lives. Then the creation He develops within us touches others.

Holly Miller, travel editor of the *Saturday Evening Post*, experienced this yielding in her own life as she grew to recognize the work God wanted to accomplish through her.

"I've learned that the areas in which I seem to be able to 'make a difference,'" comments Holly, "aren't at all what I would have suspected a few years ago. In college I wanted to be an investigative journalist who uncovers and rights all the wrongs of the world.

"But I quickly learned that I was pretty mediocre at asking unfriendly questions and putting people on the spot. Not that there isn't a place for this—but it's not my place."

As a result, Holly chose to follow God's leading in her life, and He seemed to be encouraging her to use her skills and talents to invest in the leadership of the next generation. With a master's degree in journalism from Ball State University, she devotes her life to writing and, as an adjunct professor at Anderson University, has received many professional awards and honors.

"I worry about the attitudes, beliefs, and values of the next generation of leaders. Each of us needs to figure out our own gifts—what we're good at—and concentrate on expanding and sharing these gifts.

"I've learned to try to stay focused and not become fragmented. I can't be all things to all people, and I don't want to try. Once we've determined our place, we need to concentrate in that area. I'll let Diane Sawyer and Sam Donaldson uncover the ills of society. I'll concern myself with helping to develop leaders who can correct society's problems."

Identifying God's Purpose for Your Life

God is sovereign. He is aware of every event in your life, and He uses every aspect to fulfill His purposes for your good and His glory. Take a moment and fill in the following personal inventory. Do you see any patterns? What areas have developed while other areas of interest lay dormant, waiting for the appropriate time to flourish? What areas need reconsideration? What areas have served their purpose, moving you from one stage of growth to another?

PERSONAL GIFTS, SKILLS, AND TALENTS INVENTORY

1. List talents, abilities, and skills you developed as a child. (i.e., learned to play a musical instrument, advised friends when asked, played on the football team, or came up with creative ideas for school events).

2. How are these influencing your time investment now? How have these early skills contributed to the work or activities in which you are presently involved?

3. What is your most enjoyable activity?

4. What activity do you enjoy the least?

5. If you could do anything in the world, what would you do? (This helps you determine the deeper desires of your heart.)

6. Do you feel that you are using your time economically, allowing yourself to use the gifts, talents, and abilities God has given you for His glory and the advancement of His Kingdom?

7. How could you change your schedule so that your time is invested in being the person and doing the things God has uniquely designed you to be and do?

I created a personal proverb. It is a truth that I believe in so completely, it can be put on my tombstone when I die. I contend, "There is no waste in God's economy." There is no event, situation, person, circumstance, or moment that occurs in our lives that God does not transform into a holy moment when we belong to Him. Invariably, as I observe my life, I realize there is nothing that has ever occurred that God has not been able to use. Whether gift, talent, ability, tragedy, or joy, each has equipped me to know Him better, help another know Him better, or accomplish tasks that He desired to fulfill through me.

Using God's Resources for His Glory

Have you looked at your life from that perspective? If every event and aspect of your life were part of a toolbox of resources that God desires to use for His purposes, what tools would be in your box? Are you using them? Are there some which should lie dormant to be used in the future? Which ones have lain dormant too long and need to be cleaned, polished, and prepared for God's service? Are there ones that have already served their purposes? Ones that need to be kept as a reminder of God's faithfulness and an encouragement to act in the future? Remember the parable of the talents?

It's also like a man going off on an extended trip. He called his servants together and delegated responsibilities. To one he gave five thousand dollars, to another two thousand, to a third one thousand, depending on their abilities. Then he left. Right off, the first servant went to work and doubled his master's investment. The second did the same. But the man with the single thousand dug a hole and carefully buried his master's money.

After a long absence, the master of those three servants came back and settled up with them. The one given five thousand showed him how he had doubled his investment. His master commended him: "Good work! You did your job well. From now on be my partner."

The servant given one thousand dollars said, "Master, I know you have high standards and hate careless ways, that you demand the best and make no allowances for error. I was afraid I might disappoint you, so I found a good hiding place and secured your money. Here it is, safe and sound down to the last cent."

The Master was furious. "That's a terrible way to live! It's criminal to live cautiously like that! If you knew I was after the best, why did you do less than the least? The least you could have done would have been to invest the sum with the bankers, where at least I would have gotten a little interest. Take the thousand and give it to the one who risked the most."

MATTHEW 25:14–29, THE MESSAGE

God desires that we use and invest our abilities in the advancement of His Kingdom. The servant who hid the money did so because of a distorted understanding of God. His misconceptions kept him from being used for God's glory. It's so important that our concept of God be consistent with His Word. Then we are able to risk much because we love much.

Take time now to talk with God about these things. Ask Him to show you what He is accomplishing in your life at present. Ask God to reveal your strengths developed in the past which He desires to use in the future. Seek to invest your life in things that matter to Him.

Here are examples of people who have taken the experiences and training of their pasts to make investments that are reaping eternal dividends:

Carole Johnson prays and sews to make a difference. After making dresses for children within her church, she began sewing for girls in Appalachia, the coal mining district of West Virginia and eastern Kentucky where the unemployment rate is over fifty percent.

Registered nurse Lisa Hudson began a hospital-based outreach to widows and divorcees in Augusta, Georgia. In response to the brutal killing of her own husband, a victim of terrorist bombing in Beirut, Lisa began a support group of widows and divorcees in need of love and encouragement. The group grew until soon Lisa launched a newsletter and Bible study in her home.[1]

John and Gail Wessells travel to hospitals, homes, and nursing homes and sing for comatose patients and their families. They listen with understanding to the family members of brain-injured patients. For approximately thirty minutes, they share a worship experience with patients and friends. "We're just going to worship the Lord with you," John explains to one mother.

Fifty-year-old Cookie Rodriquez and her husband run Street Academy, a warehouse turned into a school and church for gang members in Dallas. A former gang member and heroin addict, Cookie proclaims the transforming power of Jesus Christ. "I went to the streets to love."[2]

Nicole Ludlum is a mentor to a twenty-year-old woman who has been pregnant five times and is currently trying to be a mom to just one of her children. "One of her babies died and the other three are adopted or in foster care. I'm a part of a ministry called 'Teens as Parents.'"[3]

Rusty Stephens left a promising and lucrative career as a naval officer to work full time with military men and women, discipling and preparing them to labor among those who don't know Christ.[4]

These Christians have taken the unique experiences and abilities God provided and allowed Him to redeem them for eternal investment.

CHAPTER NINE

ACTIONS SPEAK LOUDER THAN WORDS

Actions speak louder than words.
Do yours consistently communicate biblical truth?
Learn how to identify and eliminate personal contradictions as you
become more conformed to the image of God's Son.
Then people will see Jesus in you.

Great is the Lord *and most worthy of praise; . . . One generation*
will commend your works to another;
they will tell of your mighty acts.

Psalm 145:3-4

*B*uddy Childress tells the story of his first career after college.
"Hard-driving, money-hungry business person describes me perfectly." He climbed the corporate ladder fast and furiously before
realizing that God had a better idea. God invited him to invest his
life in His business instead. Buddy and his family headed for
Gordon-Conwell Theological Seminary assuming God wanted
Buddy to become a church pastor.

Little did he know that God had a different plan. Early in the
second semester at seminary, it became clear to him that his
ministry wasn't in the pulpit but in the pew. The business community he knew so well needed him. They needed the life-changing
truth of Jesus Christ.

"It began to be a topic of discussion and preparation for my
wife and me. We'd never heard of a ministry to white collar workers
in the marketplace. Later we learned of three throughout the
United States, one a Pittsburgh experiment, The Citadel Mission,
and a third group meeting in the nation's capital known as "the
Fellowship."

After graduation in 1977, his hometown became his mission
field. Using his training and administrative background, he approached the Chamber of Commerce to acquire a list of business-
men in the community. From this list he identified one or two top
executives from the city's major employers and corporations. His
adventure began.

> As a minister to the business community, I called or drop-
> ped into their offices. I talked to the executives and made
> appointments for a future visit. I began to make myself available
> to some of the people and decision-makers. I didn't go into the

office to beat them over the head with the Bible or spiritual issues.

I laugh because the closing ratio of appointments was even higher than when I was in business selling. I sold the ministry to them and they bought it. I don't know if these people thought they might go to hell if they didn't see me, or what.

What I basically said was, "We're here. You're the important part of the business, and we're a ministry to your community. I want you to know we are available and have some things you might want to take advantage of."

I called the ministry "Needle's Eye" from Matthew 19:24, 26b. "It is easier for a camel to go through the eye of a needle than for a rich man to enter the kingdom of God . . . but with God, all things are possible." A local church permitted me to use a small chapel upstairs in an impressive historic church in town, and I began holding simple fifteen-minute services during lunch break. We'd have a couple of hymns and perhaps five minutes of prayer with a short sermon. At first on a good day, ten to thirty people would show up.

Growing ever since, the ministry now includes monthly luncheons featuring local business and professional people, weekly small groups, a Bible study every Friday morning in a local restaurant, a pastor's seminar called "Marketplace Trends" to enable local clergy to talk with business people about current issues they struggle with daily, and Needle's Eye '911,' an emergency service to help struggling businesses solve internal problems and keep from going under.

Taking Action for God

One man, Buddy Childress, took the resources he acquired in the setting he understood and allowed God to use him to shape an entire community. Why is he having such an impact? Because he is applying Christian principles in a secular environment. God's Word works. All those in Needle's Eye seek to act in a manner consistent with their beliefs. Actions really do speak louder than words. Particularly in the business community, a Christian who acts with integrity consistent with biblical truth stands out in the crowd. And apparently not a lot of Christians are really doing this.

"Are you part of a Christian business or are you just a Christian doing business?" appears to be an appropriate question.

John R. Crawford, a Christian writing in *WORLD* magazine, says, "Experience has taught us that Christian businesses overall are no better than secular businesses at paying their bills. One counselor advised, 'If you get a check from a ministry, run with it to the nearest bank!'"

Crawford reminds business leaders, "Only tell the world you a have a 'Christian business' if you can stand by that affirmation in service, cleanliness, honesty, and in willingness to go the extra mile to make certain that your company's work is above question."[1]

Whatever we do, wherever we go, the importance of biblically consistent actions can't be underestimated. Do your actions emulate the belief system you profess?

———

Catherine stood stunned. Sally and Catherine had been friends for years. They had worked side by side in their given profession. Competition had never been a problem. Both were interior decorators wanting to have a Christian impact in their fields. Sally, Catherine, and a third friend met monthly to exchange ideas and reward successes. Each needing the encouragement, they anticipated these times with joy and expectation.

When Catherine's career soared, Sally acted as if it didn't matter. When they spoke, Catherine knew she spoke of her success too often, but who could she share her joy with if not with her best friend? Sometimes her enthusiasm was overwhelming, but Sally seemed to join in her happiness. They rejoiced in what God was doing through them. Then one day everything changed.

Sally approached a client with a decorating idea she was excited about. Before her appointment she excitedly told Catherine all about it. Catherine hugged her and told her she'd pray for her success. This would be a real winner if Sally got the job.

Later that day, Catherine sipped tea at a local tearoom with this same client, a longtime friend. While Catherine and the client were deep in conversation, Sally passed by. They both greeted her warmly. A suspicious, shocked expression swept over Sally's face. Catherine dismissed Sally's look, unsure of its meaning.

Later, Sally appeared at Catherine's front door. Catherine greeted her cheerfully and invited her in. Noticing her cool manner, Catherine offered Sally a cup of tea. Sally refused. Finally Catherine asked what was wrong.

Sally told her everything she felt. She'd seen Catherine whispering secretively to the client at lunch. She adamantly accused Catherine of stealing her client and altering her ideas just enough to make the sale.

The hurt Catherine felt was indescribable as the smile washed from her face.

"Sally, I can't believe you are saying these things to me. I can't believe you would think these things. I would never betray our friendship by doing anything to hurt you. I know I've experienced a lot of successes lately, but certainly not at your or anyone else's expense.

"I can't help it if God is blessing what I am doing. Could it be that your jealousy has blinded your eyes to the truth? Don't you know that no client or sale would ever be worth losing your friendship?"

Sally stared straight ahead. She was sure she was right, and no amount of explaining on Catherine's part would change her opinion. Catherine asked her forgiveness for anything she could have done that precipitated Sally's feeling this way. Sally said she forgave her, but over time it was obvious that she held a grudge. The damage was irreparable; a precious friendship was lost.

Actions graphically illustrate what we believe. Sally's Christianity seemed genuine, but there was a severe breakdown in her belief system. Why was she unwilling to forgive a friend?

Something was so deeply wrong that she was unable to draw on the Holy Spirit's power to open her mind and forgive her innocent friend. When our actions do not demonstrate our Christian principles and beliefs, God's truth is hindered. We communicate something other than Christ's will and Word.

All of us have areas in our lives inconsistent with what we profess and what we live. Our hearts' desire though should be to recognize and eliminate these inconsistencies while offering mercy to those who, like us, struggle with their own blindness.

To refuse to reconcile and restore a relationship with another Christian refutes God's Word. "All this is from God, who reconciled us to himself through Christ and gave us the ministry of reconciliation: that God was reconciling the world to himself in Christ, not counting men's sins against them. And he has committed to us the message of reconciliation. We are therefore Christ's ambassadors, as though God were making his appeal through us" (2 Cor. 5:18–20). Jesus did not hold our sins against us but died to forgive us. We are His representatives acting to reach others with this same forgiveness and love.

All of us seek to represent Christ to the world with actions consistent with our beliefs. We fail often, but God's mercy through forgiveness gives us the grace to go on. As we develop the gifts God has given, offering them back to Him to be used to reach the world in His name, He will continue to mold our lives into His image. We are to be image-bearers of God. "So God created man in his own image, in the image of God he created him" (Gen. 1:27).

My dear friend Susan McKinney, dying of cancer, said often, "I'm really upset when everybody quotes Romans 8:28 without acknowledging His purpose in verse 29." In Romans 8:28 we read the familiar passage, 'And we know that in all things God works for the good of those who love him, who have been called according to his purpose.' But why does He do this? 'For those God foreknew he also predestined to be conformed to the likeness [image] of his Son, that he might be the firstborn among many brothers.'"

God constantly works in our lives with the sole purpose of transforming us to think, look, and act like Jesus. It's an impossible task. So He actually does it in and through us by the power of His Holy Spirit.

Eugene Peterson describes this transformation well in *The Message*.

> God knew what He was doing from the very beginning. He decided from the outset to shape the lives of those who love Him along the same lines as the life of his Son. The Son stands first in the line of humanity he restored. We see the original and intended shape of our lives there in him.

After God made that decision of what his children should be like, he followed it up by calling people by name. After he called them by name, he set them on a solid basis with himself. And then, after getting them established, he stayed with them to the end, gloriously completing what he had begun.

Who is doing all the work? God. Can God fail? No. So when you fail to image God's Son, and your actions do not accurately communicate your thoughts and heart, remember God waits ready to forgive, restore, and continue His work in you.

The time has come. Are you ready to ask God to help you invest your life in things that matter by identifying those actions in your life that are inconsistent with His truth? Are you ready to allow Him to begin His process of correcting the flaws? You can't go wrong. He promises His plans are good for you, "'For I know the plans I have for you,' declares the Lord, 'plans to prosper you and not to harm you, plans to give you a hope and a future'" (Jer. 29:11).

TAKING ACTION

Steps to Identify and Correct Inconsistencies

1. Ask the Holy Spirit to guide you into His truth, revealing incidents where your actions contradict your declared beliefs.

2. Look at these experiences honestly. List each and write next to the incident the applicable biblical truth. Then note the inconsistency between the biblical truth and your action. Finally, identify the action you could take the next time a similar incident arises, or if possible take the opportunity to rectify your previous action.

   Example: Yesterday your neighbor asked you to do a favor, but you refused. You said you didn't have time. Biblical truth that applies: "Love your neighbor as yourself." "Do not lie to one another."

Inconsistencies:

+ You lied about not having time. You could have adjusted your schedule and made time.

+ Realize that you love yourself enough that you would have done this thing for yourself. Why couldn't you do it for your neighbor?

Biblically Consistent Actions:

+ Gladly adjust your schedule for the sake of your neighbor, seeing this opportunity as a God-appointment to be a witness to your neighbor.

+ Explain to your neighbor that though this would be inconvenient at this time, you'd like to do it later. Take a rain check.

3. Pray that the Holy Spirit will show you your tendencies toward biblical inconsistency in certain areas and ask Him to warn you before you make incorrect choices. Then listen to His prompting as He instructs you in the responses and actions you can make.

Sometimes the truth hurts. We don't like to hear it. Sometimes the truth hurts because God uses it to perform deep, permanent "surgery" in our hearts, a surgery that ultimately is our only path to healing. Even though the truth hurts, it always ensures a profitable conclusion. We become more like Jesus and more useful to God.

Won't you begin today to yield to the hand of the Great Physician? Then you can begin to make a difference with eternal implications.

The following women are examples of those who have taken action in their community. As you read these quotes, pray about actions the Holy Spirit might be leading you to take as you demonstrate your faith to others.

Christians Taking Action

"I have a small love fund I have established in order to provide Bibles to abused, neglected women in order to encourage them to learn about God."

JOANNE RICHARDS

"I'm actively involved in fighting abortion and writing to my leaders in state and national government."

MARCIA CORRELL

"I operate a home daycare and I have learned—am learning—God's unconditional love. The outreach is incredible. Two or three of my moms come to church with me and are seeking God."

JENNIFER DONLEY

"I am currently leading a discipleship Bible study with women who are new believers and are in their mid-thirties."

LANI STEPHENS

"I'm involved in following up with unchurched children and families who attend our Vacation Bible School."

CATHY LOWDER

"Our family spent two years as missionaries in Japan. I'm now working part-time in my home producing a bimonthly newsletter to mobilize prayer for the team we worked with there as well as for the church and people of Japan."

EILEEN LASO

CHAPTER TEN

HANDLING THE RISKS
OF INVESTMENT

*How do you handle risk? Risk is an integral part of the Christian
life. Risks of faith require secure dependence on God. Is this an area
you'd like to grow in? Take this opportunity to consider risk and its
value for your life.*

*So we agreed to choose some men and send them to you with our
dear friends Barnabas and Paul—men who have risked their lives
for the name of our Lord Jesus Christ.*

ACTS 15:25–26

Damian Prince is three years old, and he is dying. He may last another week. Or a few months. Maybe even a year or more.

But he will die.

Rosa Prince cradles her grandson on her lap and tells the sad, short story of his life while he nibbles on a potato chip.

He contracted HIV at birth and developed AIDS within eighteen months. He weighs twenty pounds and walks with a limp. But he's a fighter, and so is his grandma.

In 1991, she lost her twenty-nine-year-old adopted daughter, Daisy, to AIDS. Daisy's legacy to Damian was that he, too, will die of AIDS. Again, Rosa will be there to comfort someone she loves until he can be comforted no more.

She knows the man who brought AIDS to her family through sex with her daughter. "He was a boyfriend of Daisy's," she says, and she still sees him around town. "He knows [Damian's] condition," she says. "He doesn't volunteer anything or any help at all."

Five years after her first encounter with AIDS, Rosa is not the same person.

"This disease got so big and so wide and so close and so hurtful," she says, "you don't have time to hate."

She faced the death of her daughter and the infection of her grandson. She watched her only brother, another AIDS victim, lie in a coma.

"You can be embarrassed about it and not do anything and wait and put flowers on their grave," she says, "but that doesn't help anything. The best thing to do is just roll up your sleeves and just jump right in."[1]

Rosa risked all for love. That love superseded fear of death, rejection, embarrassment, the humiliation of others' opinions, and the inevitable pain that was to come. That love looked beyond the superficial and invested in what counts—the souls and hearts of hurting people.

Investing our lives in things that matter involves risk. Walking with God is risky business. Everyday life experiences are specific appointments with God. Every event counts. The study of His Word and fellowship with Him demonstrates that He orchestrates every event, circumstance, and experience of life. He transforms life experiences into His plan of action. We are challenged to trust Him in a way that enables us to take the risks necessary to follow Him.

Are you up for the challenge? It doesn't have to be a scary thing. Fear arises when we forget the character of God. Fear comes from the feeling that means stepping out into oblivion—nothingness. And that's Satan's lie. He uses it to cripple us so we can't follow God with confidence.

Risking is stepping into the unknown, but that which is completely known by God. Stepping into the unknown does not mean stepping into oblivion. It means stepping into the known will of God—something you may not see right now as tangible but something more real than life itself. It requires stepping into His hand—the trusted hand of a faithful friend.

Stepping into God's Hand

God's Word gives us the knowledge of His person. The promises of His Word are our security and assurance. Isaiah voices God's heart in chapter 51:12–13, 15–16:

> "I, even I, am he who comforts you.
> Who are you that you fear mortal men,
> the sons of men, who are but grass,
> that you forget the LORD your Maker,
> who stretched out the heavens and laid the
> foundations of the earth, . . .
> For I am the LORD your God,
> who churns up the sea so that its waves roar—
> the LORD Almighty is his name.

I have put my words in your mouth
    and covered you with the shadow of my hand—
I who set the heavens in place,
    who laid the foundations of the earth,
    and who say to Zion, 'You are my people.'"

Knowing the character and hand of God is the first step in risking. Moses and David both knew that hand. Moses sings with Miriam,

"Your right hand, O LORD,
    was majestic in power.
Your right hand, O LORD,
    shattered the enemy.
In the greatness of your majesty
    you threw down those who opposed you."

EXODUS 15:6–7

David rests secure.

If the LORD delights in a man's way,
    he makes his steps firm;
though he stumble, he will not fall,
    for the LORD upholds him with his hand.

PSALM 37:23–24

Why does the Christian life involve risk? Because everything seems risky when our natural instincts are opposed. God's ways and thoughts are not our own. Often, the directions of His will seem unnatural and uncomfortable. That's because they are supernatural. The Spirit of God is the only one who can give us the power to complete them. His directions are supernatural and must be supernaturally fulfilled by the power of the Holy Spirit.

Taking the Risk

Rob Schermerhorn, operations manager at Blue Ridge Broadcasting, Black Mountain, North Carolina, understands risk. An administrator at the Billy Graham radio station, WFGW/WMIT, Rob believes that one of the most exciting parts of the Christian life is trying something you've never tried before.

> So many people are afraid to try something new—something they've never done before. For example, when I first became Operations Manager, my job had a very narrow scope. I did my job to the best of my ability but began to imagine creative ways to try new things which would enhance the station's outreach.

> I attempted things never considered before to meet needs I recognized. Designing and supervising construction on building remodeling and expansion were things I'd never tried before. But I was willing. As every new idea and area of interest developed and the scope of my job broadened, the opportunities for meeting needs creatively were enormous.

> Whatever you choose to invest in—take a risk. Jump out of your box of limited experiences and possibilities into things totally new. When you're within God's will you can do anything. Then He expands the scope and dimensions of the box.

Relying on God's resources alone because you know, without a shadow of a doubt, that yours are insufficient, paves the way for risk-taking. Our resources are always insufficient. Jesus tells us, "Apart from me you can do nothing" (John 15:5). But at times we have difficulty admitting this to ourselves and others. The more we rely on God alone in every aspect of life, the more we experience His power. Unfortunately this fact often seems to escape us. We suffer from spiritual weakness as a result.

Trusting His Character

The second step in taking risks is not only *knowing* but *trusting* the character of God. You can know all there is to know about God and not place your trust in Him. God desires that we lean on Him literally, relying and clinging to Him for all we do and say. Then He is able to work through us and use us to accomplish His purposes. We begin a life of investing in things that matter. This is Paul's message. "But we have this treasure in jars of clay to show that this all-surpassing power is from God and not from us" (2 Cor. 4:7).

When we yield our lives to God and are willing to risk the humanly impossible to accomplish the supernaturally possible, He is the one recognized. People see God's face through our own. This is God's desire—that others will see Him and come to know Him so they may spend eternity with Him.

Choosing His Will

You've heard people bemoan their plight with the words, "This is my cross to bear." They refer to some daily suffering such as a rebellious child, an alcoholic husband, or a crippling disease. These inferences are a distortion of the true meaning of Jesus' words, "If anyone would come after me, he must deny himself and take up his cross and follow me" (Matt. 16:24). What cross are we to carry? Certainly Jesus is not referring to the wooden cross He carried to His death.

No, Christ's cross symbolizes His death in payment for our life, a sacrificial death by choice. Jesus chose to die. In His humanity it was not something He wanted to do; it was an act of the will to yield to the Father's desire. Graphically portrayed with His words, "Father, if you are willing, take this cup from me"(Luke 22:42), Jesus dreaded the death He was about to suffer. *The Message* translates Jesus' words here, "My Father, if there is any way, get me out of this. But please not what I want. You, what do you want?"

He chose His Father's will over the deliverance His flesh so desired. To follow the Father's will, Jesus chose to take up His cross, dying to His will to follow the Father's will. Our cross is the same. It is our decision. Are we willing to die to our fleshly desires and choose God's will over our own?

The story of James Calvert illustrates the meaning of Jesus' words. When James Calvert went out as a missionary to the cannibals of the Fiji Islands, the captain of the ship tried to stop him by saying, "You will lose your life and the lives of those with you if you go among such savages." Calvert's reply demonstrated the reality of commitment to the will of God. "We died before we came here."[2]

We may immediately assume that all risks of faith are dangerous. Because of that fear we choose self-protective attitudes and actions. Joyce Wilson, a pastor's wife in Hopewell, Virginia, writes, "We isolate ourselves in our holy huddles to the place that we have little contact with the outside world." Biblical texts that warn Christians to avoid the world's influence such as "Do not love the world or anything in the world" (1 John 2:15), and "Do not conform any longer to the pattern of this world" (Rom. 12:2) are used as excuses for non-action.

For some of us simply telling a stranger about Jesus takes a great deal of courage and reliance on the Holy Spirit because we fear rejection. Jesus understands our hesitancy. He does not scorn or demean us for our fears. But He expects us to come to Him to remove them. He reminds us that His perfect love casts out *all* fear. He assists us with His power to do His will as we trust Him. Trusting Him with small steps of faith prepares us to know His presence and to act with assurance when the opportunity for large steps arise.

Carolyn Hall found this to be true. Urban chaos and racial unrest typify Carolyn's life. She chose to do something about it. Having witnessed the Birmingham, Alabama, urban crisis in the sixties and the Watts riots in California, Carolyn and her husband moved from a safe area in Los Angeles nine years ago to settle in the heart of a community that smoldered with crime, poverty, and gang wars. There they established the Lighthouse Christian Fellowship, a non-denominational church that feeds their community's stomach and souls.

Carolyn said, "Pain is like a cancer. It spreads. It festers. But understanding and sharing is the cure. It begins with each one of us." What can be done to ease the tension and anger? "We've been praying a lot for those in authority—for God to give them divine guidance. We pray that they surround themselves with praying people. We pray for restoration to come back. We're praying that relations begin to be mended.

"I constantly tell myself, God has not given me the spirit of fear, but of power and love and a sound mind."[3]

Whatever risks God may be asking you to take, He will give you His presence and the power to do it.

Trusting God's Weaving

Taking risks also involves trusting God's sovereign ability to work everything together for your best and His good. Fear is eliminated when you realize that no matter what happens as a result of taking a risk of faith, God will weave it into your life and the lives of others in a positive way.

God is the author and source of good. God's will is always good. He knows what is good when we don't. Genesis describes this clearly and repeatedly, "And God saw that it was good" (Gen. 1:12). We may look at a situation or event in our lives and say, "Lord, this is *not good*." His response is, "Trust me. I know what is good when you don't and I am working out everything into that which is good for you and Me both."

Paul powerfully explains God's method of accomplishing His will in our lives. "In him we were also chosen, having been predestined according to the plan of him *who works out everything in conformity with the purpose of his will*, in order that we, who were the first to hope in Christ, might be for the praise of his glory" (Eph. 1:11–12). He weaves everything into the fabric of our lives so that His will is accomplished.

For some churches, branching out into new aspects of ministry involves risk. One man willing to risk everything to be in the will of God is Bill Hybels, pastor of Willow Creek Church in Chicago. What caused him to take risks that thrust his church into the evangelical spotlight as a church on the cutting edge of the next century?

A simple door-to-door survey precipitated his innovative and highly untraditional approach to church ministry. After conducting this survey throughout the west Chicago suburbs, he and his friends made some startling discoveries. He discovered that most who refuse to attend church had four reasons. They believed

1. churches were always asking for money;
2. the services were boring and routinely predictable;
3. church had no relevance to real life;
4. pastors made attenders feel guilty or stupid.

Based on these opinions, Hybels and his team developed a church experience that defied these assumptions. They began meeting in a movie theater, attempting to create a "safe place" for the unchurched to hear a "dangerous sermon" as Hybels puts it.

"Our goal is to reach and teach 'non-churched' Harrys and Marys who have been turned off by traditional church and are about to write off Christianity," Bill remarks. "Seekers can be anonymous here . . . You don't have to say anything, sing anything, sign anything, or give anything."[4]

Taking risks paid off. God honored Bill's obedience and not only is this church thriving, but many have applied his methods to begin vital ministries throughout the United States.

Just Do It!

Finally, risk-taking demands obedience to God's Word, and the direction He gives as the Holy Spirit personally applies the Word in our lives. We've discussed thinking biblically and knowing what you believe. We've explored aspects of communicating our beliefs through attitudes and actions. Developing our gifts, identifying the risks, overcoming fear with faith in God's character, and learning to trust follow. Then it's up to us to, "Just do it!" Obey the Lord. Step out and trust God's undergirding hand. Risk the impossible knowing that with God all things are possible.

God has been speaking to you as you've read this chapter. What are the risks of faith He is encouraging you to take? Take a moment now and review the "Steps to Handling Risk" below and pray for wisdom. God will show you where you are in His process of risk-taking and give you the power to move forward. More important is your desire to say "yes" to whatever God asks. He will never lead you where He has not gone before you. Trust Him.

STEPS TO HANDLING THE RISKS

1. *Know the character of God.* Study His Word to discover His character. Saturate yourself in the assurance that He will never change. His character of love, faithfulness, mercy,

grace, and goodness will always be active on your behalf. When you step out in faith you are not stepping into oblivion but into the trusted hand of God.

2. *Trust His character.* You can know everything about God and never choose to trust Him. Trust is taking risks believing that you can depend on His character and Word. You have the assurance He can be trusted. As you exercise your faith, it will grow when God acts faithfully on your behalf.

3. *Choose His will over your own.* This process will repeat itself every day of your life. It will take a conscious decision and direct act of your will. Your sinful nature resists trusting God and choosing His will. You may innately believe that you know what is best, and you may not trust another to make decisions for you. This is totally human. You may assume that no other person can have your best interests at heart.

   God does. The one who knows all things, understands all things, and has the power to do something about all things certainly can be trusted to guide and direct your life. Why not choose to follow His direction at the expense of dying to your own will and desires? It's the best choice you will ever make.

4. *Depend on His weaving.* As you step out to make decisions consistent with God's Word and will, God will weave together every detail of your life to produce His perfect will. Even when you blow it, He redeems the mess when you return to Him. That's your promise. "Therefore, I urge you, brothers, in view of God's mercy, to offer your bodies as living sacrifices, holy and pleasing to God—this is your spiritual act of worship. Do not conform any longer to the pattern of this world, but be transformed by the renewing of your mind. Then you will be able to test and approve what God's will is—his good, pleasing and perfect will" (Rom. 12:1–2).

5. *JUST DO IT!!* Obey God with abandon. You can trust Him. This investment strategy will never fail.

PART THREE

Getting
---
the Word Out:

How Do You Do It?
---

*T*hroughout this book we have discussed the very personal aspects of investing our lives in things that matter. Biblical consistency in your personal life, thoughts, attitudes, and actions highlight the pages. Integrating the truth of God's Word into every aspect of your personal life should be of primary concern. Then you can begin to discuss your investment in the lives of others.

God's Word and people who will join us in heaven are the only eternally significant two things. By following the investment of God's Word in our personal lives, we can shift our focus to the investment of God's Word through us into the lives of others. The power of influence cannot be underestimated. Whether you know it or not you're exerting that power every day. Family, friends, neighbors, passing acquaintances, relatives, and all those you meet are being affected by your life.

As you mentor, nurture, love, and grow in fellowship with your most intimate acquaintances, you build relationships that provide the building blocks for communicating your integrated biblical world and life view to those you care about most. This is the thrust of this section. How can you most effectively invest in the lives of those you love? Turn the page and we'll continue this pilgrimage.

CHAPTER ELEVEN

THE POWER OF INFLUENCE

You are a leader. Someone is watching and following your example whether you realize it or not. How can you positively influence those closest to you for Jesus Christ? How can you lead them to a deeper walk with God? Explore the dimensions of your influence in the relationships God brings into your life.

Be very careful, then, how you live—not as unwise but as wise,
making the most of every opportunity, because the days are evil.
Ephesians 5:15–16

*W*aiting for my friend is never a problem. I always attempt to
arrive before she does so as not to cause her to wait. Her small,
trim, seventy-year-old figure slips from the car when she arrives.
She greets me with a hug. Graying blond hair is tied back into a
ponytail at the nape of her neck, and her clothing speaks of
understated refinement. But her most striking features are her
sparkling blue eyes and vibrant smile.

As we chat comfortably at lunch, I'm sure this woman is
unaware of the influence she has had on my life. We simply meet
for lunch. I share concerns I have as a pastor's wife, speaker, and
writer. She, too, is the wife of a husband in full-time ministry. She
responds with fascinating stories of her life and interests that give
me perspective and advice. She, too, is a writer. Her gracious
kindness and wisdom never cease to touch me. Her life has not been
easy. My friend is Ruth Graham.

Another friend comes to mind. Tall, statuesque, also refined in her
appearance with a beauty that radiates from within, confidence
exudes from this woman. She speaks only after careful thought,
and her words are exacting. They hit the mark precisely as she
communicates truth she is learning or poses questions so as to
know my thoughts and ideas.

I first met this woman when I was a young student anxious to
learn more about writing. Her seminary course on Christian communication was one I would never forget. The content captivated
me, but the woman who articulated it held even greater interest. I
often tell others she is the most uncompromising woman I have

ever met. She is a spokeswoman for our generation, challenging us to sacrificial and unflinching commitment to God.

This woman's influence on my life remains consistent. She, too, probably continues to be unaware of her role in God's plan for me. My friend is Elisabeth Elliot.

───────

Another woman cannot be overlooked. Warm, loving, generous, bold in communicating ideas and also unwavering in her beliefs, this woman maintains the most marked influence in my life. Always my cheerleader, encouraging and supporting when all others seem to disappear, this woman's influence permeates every aspect of my life and ministry. This friend, my best friend, is my mother.

───────

Using Influence for Christ

The power of influence astounds me. Whether positively or negatively, we influence every person we meet. Christ's method of leadership was influence. Disciples, family, friends, religious leaders, and government authorities listened to His words but marveled at His life. His life served to underscore the truth of His words, the two being utterly consistent.

Influence and its accompanying term, "mentoring," grab a lot of attention in the Christian community. Disaster often strikes Christians when influence and mentoring grow vague. Generations of disciples flounder for solid moorings in an otherwise unstable world. When the foundational truth of God's Word is not implanted deep in the heart and modeled by the lives of respected leaders, followers lose their way. They wander and stray like sheep lost in the forest. Sin crouches ready to seize them. Many are ensnared.

Leighton Ford Ministries recognizes the imperative need for mentoring in the building of disciples and seeks to address this problem. Tom Hawks, director of Leadership Training for Leighton Ford Ministries, fervently asserts,

> Our culture is experiencing an intense generational gap in leadership. There are the older entrepreneurial leaders such as

Billy Graham and the emerging leaders in their thirties, but leaders in the forty to fifty age group are few. The natural mentoring that those in the later group would offer younger men and women isn't happening. We at Leighton Ford Ministries are attempting to bridge that gap. We attempt to supply the missing ingredients that this natural mentoring would otherwise supply.

There is a polarity among young leaders. Many excel in vision, organization, and communication skills yet their walk with God is shaky. Those who are mature in their relationship with God, familiar with Scripture, have a vibrant prayer life, etc. often lack the skills of the first group. Our desire is to blend the abilities of both, equipping each in their area of need. We call it a "wedding of character and competency."

How do they accomplish this?

In our two-year program, twenty to twenty-five men and women are selected from throughout the U.S. to participate in the program. They fly to Charlotte for in-house seminars held here twice a year and in between these times, they meet with mentors, complete assignments and are involved with area peer groups.

Four broad areas of study are examined. Spiritual formation is the first, encouraging each to rely on God rather than on their own skills and abilities. Here they see God's work accomplished through His efforts. The second area, leadership, addresses the acquiring of skills, values, attitudes consistent with the ultimate leadership model, Jesus Christ.

The third area is personal evangelism. We believe every Christian leader needs to develop an increasing concern for those outside the believing community. Finally, the fourth area is kingdom seeking, mobilizing the church to seek kingdom growth worldwide.

Does this seem a little overwhelming? It's really not. Each of us is a leader. Someone is watching and following our example regardless of our opinion about that fact. Tom names significant areas we can consider for personal growth and development. If mentoring and influence are unavoidable, wouldn't it be better to choose to grow in these areas so that we can become more effective servants of Jesus Christ?

And that's what influence is—servant leadership. It involves relationship building, compassion, and caring. If our lives are going to affect others, why not invest in those God brings across our path by choice? Then our influence will be prayerfully exerted rather than haphazardly applied.

Let's reconsider the areas Tom mentioned. Prayerfully answer the questions in this evaluation as you consider investing in the lives you care about most, family and intimate friends.

PERSONAL INFLUENCE EVALUATION SHEET

Spiritual Formation

1. How are you seeking to grow in your relationship with God each day?
2. What tools are you applying to enhance that growth? Tools I recommend include *The Experiencing God Study Bible* and the *One-Year Bible* for daily Bible reading. The student manual from the *Women in the Word Bible* study series gives a more in-depth study of God's Word. Navigator's *Scripture Memory System* will help you store God's Word in your heart. *Experiencing God* by Henry T. Blackaby and Claude V. King will help you discover the joy of knowing and doing God's will.
3. Describe an event that illustrates growing ability to rely on God rather than your own skills and abilities (John 15:5).

Leadership

4. Describe the ways you believe you have the greatest influence on others. (Examples: decisive in your opinions, compassionate in your caring, generous in your serving)
5. How do these exemplify the servant leadership style of Jesus Christ? List verses if possible.
6. In what areas do you feel you need to grow? What can you begin doing in your personal life to stimulate this growth? (Examples: study God's Word as it applies to forgiveness if you are weak in forgiving others, study biblical references that demonstrate the ways Jesus extended love to

others if you have a difficult time being loving, learn about gentleness from God's Word if you tend to be sharp and critical.)

Personal Evangelism

7. When was the last time you told someone about Jesus Christ? Describe the event.

8. Do you know the basics of the Gospel so that you can share it concisely and succinctly when opportunity arises? (Materials available from Evangelism Explosion, P.O. Box 23820, Ft. Lauderdale, FL 33307-3820, 1-800-491-6106, provide an excellent resource for a basic Gospel presentation. They are best applied in a group setting but are available to individuals.)

9. Are you presently praying for at least three non-Christian friends, relatives, or acquaintances?

Kingdom Seeking

10. Are you active in your church world outreach program? How can you develop a growing concern for world missions? (The book *Operation World* by Patrick Johnstone is an excellent tool to help you offer daily prayer for world missions.)

11. Have you considered new ways to reach out to the internationals who live within your community? Have you entertained international students from area colleges or universities? What opportunities are available to you?

12. Do you and your family pray for those involved in the world affairs whom you watch on television or read about in the newspaper each day?

Building Relationships

How can you make a difference in the lives of those you love? Building healthy relationships is the first key. This begins with the knowledge that only God can meet the deepest needs of your heart. Desire that each person you know and love will come to a personal knowledge of Him. As each one draws on the love, compassion, security, caring, and tenderness of God, your relationships will not be an emotionally draining experience. No longer will one person attempt to have his needs met by another. Relationships will be an act of giving out of the abundance the Lord has provided. You'll find that He supplies Himself to meet your needs.

Second, pray to be sensitive to the ones who are closest to you. Are they in need today of God's touch through you? How can you be a source of encouragement and hope? Are you willing to take time to listen if they simply want to talk?

Third, awaken each morning expectantly prepared for God's plan for the day. You may have a schedule but sensitivity to God's appointments is imperative. When someone comes to your door unexpectedly or the telephone rings insistently, do you prayerfully stop to welcome God's intervention in your day?

Fourth, learn to value and cherish those around you, introducing them to qualities you recognize in them that they may be unaware of. Become a talent scout observing and identifying the qualities God has developed within an individual. Help them to see God working in their lives, and explain how God has used them to bless you and others.

Finally, pray that your attitudes and actions will not only be consistent with your beliefs but that these will be communicated to others.

I had a remarkable experience several months ago. I stop at Hardee's almost every day. Recently there was a complete change in management and staffing.

One day the woman who served me paused and blurted, "OK, what's the secret?" I was totally dumbfounded. She saw my confusion. "You know . . .what's the secret? You smile all the time. What's the secret to happiness?"

I was so surprised that I groped for a moment for an answer, and finally replied, "Jesus Christ." That was all. A little perplexed, she smiled and I drove off smiling as well. We may be completely unaware of our influence in other's lives, but the light and love of Jesus Christ flows through us when we are walking in fellowship with Him.

Relationships and Respect

In summary, relationships built on mutual respect that encourages others to grow in their gifts, talents, and expertise prove to be the most effective in reaching out to people. When you listen carefully, respond appropriately, and desire to facilitate growth in another's life, you will find your influence will be both positive and successful. You are reflecting Jesus' method. He valued and appreciated people for the those sovereignly assigned qualities that made them unique.

As your life demonstrates the life of Jesus, others will be touched and will want to emulate Him. They will mirror Him, not you, because your words and actions will be constantly giving Him glory. Scott Holmquist, Program Director at the Billy Graham Training Center, comments,

> A leader cannot be "one of the guys" in one sense. He has to be head of the sphere, at times making unpopular decisions and providing vision in new and unpopular directions.
>
> The metaphor of "coaching" becomes an effective one. The coach begins on the floor with the players, demonstrating every skill needed for the player's success. He talks through the mechanics with the player, encouraging him by repetition and demonstration until the skill is mastered. At this point, though, the coach gets off the floor. He no longer is caught up in the details. He oversees the game.
>
> Jesus did this. He always demonstrated first, then often (not always) but often explained next; then he sent them out to do it.

As we live our lives before God, our prayer can be that through us others will be influenced. As relationships grow, take any opportunity to lead others to His feet. At His feet they, too, will come to know Him more intimately and in turn lead others to Him. That's influence at its best.

CHAPTER TWELVE

INVESTING YOUR LIFE IN GOD'S PEOPLE

Investing in the body of Christ is an eternal investment.
Is the way your church functions and worships
consistent with biblical truth?
Consider Christ's desire for His Body
and evaluate fresh ways to communicate His character.

My prayer is . . . that all of them may be one, Father, just as you are in me and I am in you. May they also be in us so that the world may believe that you have sent me. I have given them the glory that you gave me, that they may be one as we are one: I in them and you in me. May they be brought to complete unity to let the world know that you sent me and have loved them even as you have loved me.

John 17:20–23

Sundresses or shorts, jeans or dress slacks, designer suits or khaki work pants, bonnets or bare heads—people of every age in every attire chatted casually in clusters as I arrived at the elementary school in York, Pennsylvania. This gathering of people from every walk of life represented the Living Word Community Church.

Led by Pastor Steve Almquist, Living Word began with a small core group of faithful members and now fills the school where they meet. Buying and renovating an empty elementary school building provided ample space and opportunity for the thriving ministry.

As I entered, area teenagers were playing basketball in the gym, Sunday School teachers were leading groups in classrooms, and worship was taking place in the remodeled cafeteria. Living Word's multifaceted approach to local church ministry was captivating.

Participation in worship was diverse as well. Guitarists and flutists introduced worship choruses. One young man stood to testify of God's protection over his family's life when their house burned to the ground.

Another spoke of God's faithfulness when a job opportunity eliminated his unemployment. People praised God while accompanied by an organ. Spontaneous praise followed as church members alternately rose to their feet. Pastor Steve's message of truth from God's Word challenged the body of believers.

My children sat transfixed as two western-dressed fifth graders gallop down the aisle on wooden "horses" inviting children to the upcoming "Adventures for Jesus" Bible school. Smiles, chuckles, and delighted whispers rewarded the actors. Musical strains closed the ninety-minute worship experience with joyous toe-tapping refrains that gave glory to God.

I felt contagious joy. My family and I wanted to return. How about you? What does it mean to be the church, the body of Christ?

Responding to the Church

How are our life investments affected by the church? How is the church affected by our investments? The most intimate associations we will experience in this life outside of those with family and dearest friends are our relationships within the body of Christ. What is our role as a member of Christ's family? What is the church's role in our pursuit of God's will for our life investments?

The question of our role in Christ's body demands our attention. God never called us to be spectators. He called us to be participants. We unite with believers to know and do the will and work of God. He never intended for us to function alone.

We know that we are to join with Christ's body because He instructs us to do so. "Let us not give up meeting together, as some are in the habit of doing, and let us encourage one another—and all the more as you see the Day approaching" (Heb. 10:25). When we believe on and receive Jesus Christ, we become a permanent part of God's family. Participation is not optional. God designed His body for our personal well-being and to ensure effectiveness in our mission to the world.

We need each other whether we like it or not. It's been said the church is the only group that shoots its own wounded. As is true of everyone, we are sinners. Because of our sin we may hurt each other either unintentionally or intentionally at times, but that does not give us an excuse to isolate ourselves from His body.

When a united group has like goals, common purposes are achieved. So we join with God's people to grow in our knowledge of Him, to be encouraged in our faith, and to receive needed support individually and as a body to accomplish His will in this generation.

Church Mission

The mission of the church, simply stated, is threefold—evangelize, assimilate, and nurture. How well is the church of Jesus Christ accomplishing the mission? How well is your local church fulfilling its calling? How well are you contributing to its success? How effectively are you investing yourself in Christ's ministry?

It is our responsibility as part of Christ's body to consider these questions on a regular basis. It is so easy to develop secure routines and practices that eventually squeeze God out of the picture. I heard someone once ask, "If the Holy Spirit were to leave your church, would He be missed? Or would you keep functioning like a well-oiled machine devoid of supernatural presence and power?"

Many are seeking God for His insight on these questions. They are willing to attempt innovative approaches to church ministry and worship so as to reach the largest number for Christ's kingdom (evangelism), incorporate people in the life of the church (assimilation), and consistently disciple them so that their knowledge and love for God grows and they in turn touch the lives of others (nurturing). This continues the cycle.

New Ways to Emulate Christ in the Church

Some may oppose new and innovative approaches to church ministry, but none can deny that Jesus went to the people where they were and touched them at their point of need. The following magazine article catches us by surprise. Its message is clear.

> All of a sudden, people are pouring back into churches and synagogues with a fervor that hasn't been seen since the fifties. It appears that a great revival is sweeping the land—until you examine the situations a little more clearly . . .
> Alcoholics? Third door to the right.
> Sex addicts? They meet on Tuesday.
> Overweight men with a problem with compulsive shopping? Pull up a chair, buddy. You're in the right place.

What is it? A support group meeting, one of many attended by fifteen million Americans each week. The authors continue,

> Most professionals and, of course, support-group members themselves, see the meetings as an amazingly effective antidote to aloneness . . . and finally Support groups are obviously based on the ancient concept of community. . . . [1]

The "ancient concept of community" referred to is God's concept, the concept of His church. A concept that the contemporary church has all but lost. There is some irony in the fact that as individuals in our culture become more isolated, it is within the church walls they seek fellowship and companionship.

But often the contemporary church is not offering the Christ who meets needy people's needs. Instead it offers a standard of performance and attitude of perfection alien to unbelievers. They enter its walls during regular services and discover rules and rituals that brand them as outcasts and outsiders. So they leave and later the church building is used to provide for groups that will offer the support they so desperately seek.

What did Jesus do? What is His example to us as we consider our role as His body? Jesus went out where the people were, touched them in their need, and taught them the truth. His methods were very unconventional for His time, just as they seem to be for ours.

As the body of Christ it *is* possible to change our methods without changing our message. Churches can be different. The only essentials are the same ones practiced by the Lord Jesus Christ and His earliest followers. What are they? Here are a few. Add others as you study and seek the Lord for your role as part of His living, functioning body.

+ "When He saw the crowds, he had compassion on them" (Matt. 9:36).

+ "He welcomed them and spoke to them about the kingdom of God" (Luke 9:11).

+ "And he took bread, gave thanks and broke it, and gave it to them, saying, 'This is my body given for you; do this in remembrance of me'" (Luke 22:19).

+ "The Son of man came eating and drinking, and they say, 'Here is . . . a friend of sinners'" (Matt. 11:19).

+ "All the believers were together and had everything in common . . . they broke bread in their homes and ate together with glad and sincere hearts, praising God and enjoying the favor of all the people" (Acts 2:44, 46–47).

✦ "Then Jesus came to them and said, 'All authority in heaven and on earth has been given to me. Therefore, go and make disciples of all nations, baptizing them in the name of the Father and of the Son and of the Holy Spirit, and teaching them to obey everything I have commanded you. And surely I am with you always, to the very end of the age" (Matt. 28:18–20).

The Church's Role in the Community

How about you? How about your church? Are you participating in these fundamental elements of church life? Are they available in your local church? If not, why not? These questions are important if your desire is to be biblically sharp and to live a life consistent with God's Word so that you may be conformed to the image of His Son.

To do this you may find it necessary to affiliate with a church body whose practices are more consistent with biblical truth. The question is not whether a church fellowship is traditional or contemporary. The question is whether it is consistent with biblical truth. You may feel assured that only to the degree that it conforms to God's Word and character, will it be effective in your life or that of others.

Win Arn of the Institute for American Church Growth said, "Some [churches] will be successful, some won't. Those that will grow will have a philosophy of ministry and a clear target audience and will build in things to make that happen. Those doing business as usual are the ones that are going to go down." He added, "The survivors will be innovators." He predicts that one of the small groups will be the affinity groups, knitted together by age, interest, and mutual marital status rather than geographical location or schedule. Focus will be the glue that holds them together.[2]

George Gallup said, "small groups are 'the most encouraging trend in religion today,' because members learn from the Bible, are taught how to pray, and are empowered for social service."[3]

James Rutz, in his compelling article "A New and Better Church," wrote, "All in all, our present church system gags, isolates, and emasculates the layman. That's why more and more Christians are walking away from the church every year. It's time for us to wake up and read the footprints. Spectator Christianity has run smack into the boomer wave—ex-hippies who STILL refuse to be folded, stapled, or mutilated."[4]

Some churches are responding to the needs of those in our culture, attempting to reach them and then teach the truth. Swift Creek Church of Richmond, Virginia, is one of these. A church-planting endeavor with worship services held in the local theater, its invitation is designed to touch local residents. A flyer mailed to hundreds of new residents in the area said: "If you are tired of carrying around burdens of anger, fear, worry, guilt, and shame due to destructive relationships—past and present, we invite you to a new kind of small group being offered here at Swift Creek."[5]

Lake Points Baptist Church of Dallas, Texas, offers a Saturday night worship service. "There is a population of unchurched people who cannot be reached by Sunday morning service," explains Mark Yoakum, minister of education. They've experienced phenomenal growth at their Sunday services, attesting to the fact that varied services are essential in the modern world.[6]

Check your reaction to new approaches to worship. Are your reactions consistent with God's Word or merely a response to traditional format and order?

YOUR RESPONSE TO INNOVATION IN THE CHURCH

1. Do you join in singing praise songs during the church service, or would you like them eliminated?
2. If a member of the congregation stands and asks for prayer for a personal problem, does it make you uncomfortable?
3. Do you shun small groups because you consider them gossip sessions?
4. Do you feel strange worshiping in any place other than a church building?
5. Do you think contemporary church music, guitar, or audio-recorder unsuitable for the Sunday worship service?

6. Do you object to the pastor using innovative methods such as drama, music, congregational participation to present the gospel?

Christ's Body Outside the Church Building

Honking horns, screeching brakes, bumper-to-bumper traffic. Braving this busy early-morning traffic, a small group of business-men meet in a downtown skyscraper each Wednesday. Called "the Fellowship," they devote an hour for prayer, studying the Bible, and discussion. They, like others, are creating opportunities to join with Christ's body outside the church building walls.

Who are these men? Lawyers, engineers, ministers, real estate executives, and bankers—a cross-section of twenty dedicated Christians.

"It goes back to John Wesley. He was the one who put together the framework for the fellowship idea," explains Jim Doherty. "In the Fellowship, part of the work is sharing the Christian walk and accountability, getting perspective from one another. We try to stay as far from being an institution or organization as possible. We feel it gets in the way of Christ."

Jim has made this early morning trip for prayer for twenty years. And his life reflects the influence. No headlines of conver-sions, no testimonials of influence, no national recognition—a quiet life of day-to-day emphasis on the things that matter. His is not a once-a-week or a spectator event commitment. He has committed his life.

Are you rightly relating to Christ's body in a way that you are not only encouraged and built up but are able to do the same for other believers? Are you joined with Christ in your desire for and the activity of reaching others for His kingdom? It's time to con-sider this aspect of your life as you proceed to invest your life in things that matter. Investing your life in the mission and work of Christ's body throughout the world will be an investment you will never regret.

CHAPTER THIRTEEN

Don't Do as the Romans Do, Just Understand How They Think

Would you like to develop practical ways to talk with non-Christians about your faith? Do you fear their anger or rejection? Develop a new understanding of the secular community so you can communicate your faith with confidence.

He is able to deal gently with those who are ignorant and are going astray, since he himself is subject to weakness. This is why he has to offer sacrifices for his own sins, as well as for the sins of the people.
Hebrews 5:2–3

Shuffling feet, clattering desks, the odor of white board markers, and the whispers of anxious students surrounded Emily Miller as she faced her first day in the college classroom. At age forty, Emily's mid-life crisis drove her back to the classroom. Flutterings like butterfly wings reminded her of her excitement. Finally, after so many years she was back in the classroom pursuing her lifelong dream of becoming a writer. The professor's brisk step announced his arrival to the class—Creative Writing 101.

Smiling at his class, Dr. Kelly made an immediate assignment. "Why do you want to write? Compose a brief paragraph to answer that question." His head dropped to look at the papers scattered on his desk and ignored the class.

Emily pulled her yellow legal pad from beneath her newly purchased books. She began to scribble her thoughts.

"Writing gives me an opportunity to express the truth. Life experiences provide the context for wisdom and insight. Communicating truth through insights I've acquired as a result of life's lessons fascinates me. That is why I want to write."

Satisfied with her paper, Emily waited patiently for the others to finish. Dr. Kelly raised his head again. He collected the papers and flipped through the pile, skimming each with an absent expression. Suddenly he stopped, reread the one on top and spoke.

"Class, listen to this." With his first words Emily realized it was her paper being read. When he finished, Dr. Kelly looked up, stared at the class, and stated firmly, "What is truth? There is no absolute truth, so it is impossible for Ms. Miller to base her desire to write or her writing career on such a belief." He slapped her composition down and picked up another.

"Now, another student writes . . . "

His voice droned on while Emily considered his response. Neither vindictive nor callused, Dr. Kelly spoke as if his words were unquestionable fact. Emily knew immediately this class was going to be both a blessing and challenge. She now had the privilege of demonstrating to Dr. Kelly concepts he had obviously never considered. Either the ideas in her compositions would be completely new to him, or he would be forced to rethink the rote philosophy he had assumed through his own education.

Maybe he would change his mind. Maybe not. But she believed God would give her the opportunity to challenge him just as she, too, had been challenged many times. Each day she'd reconsidered her beliefs as she applied them to her life's experiences. Long ago, she refused to adopt beliefs of others simply because she was expected to do so. She decided to study the truths of God's Word with new fervor, knowing that God had validated the truth of His Word in her daily experience.

She looked forward to presenting that truth to Dr. Kelly. *This class is going to be great!*, she thought with enthusiasm.

———

Do you join Emily in finding the challenge of representing truth in a secular society an exciting or threatening prospect? Respected Christian voices teach us to distrust the world and all who are a part of it. They tell us that secular society does not want to hear from those who follow Christian beliefs. And they are right. But is the world's resistance *always* a hostile one? Or is it often an uninformed and mistaken position concerning the Christian faith?

Does the world reject the God of the Bible or some misconception of God created from negative church experiences, misunderstandings of Christians, or simple uninvolvement with anyone representing the name of Christ?

In the past, society discounted anything to do with faith because it appeared intangible and, therefore, invalid. "Richard Harwood, former ombudsman [liaison] for the *Washington Post*, has speculated that poor coverage might result because as 'realists' and 'empiricists' we look on religion as we look on love and hate—too much a part of us and the world to ignore but too elusive to explore."[1]

Common thinking in past society was what cannot be touched cannot be real. In Steven Carter's book, *The Culture of Disbelief*, he says he once considered titling his book *God as a Hobby*, referring to the view that belief in God is acceptable only if it remains private and personal, "like collecting stamps or model trains."[2]

It is accurate to assume that society naturally resists the reality of God and truth. Why shouldn't it? The Bible explains, "Those who live according to the sinful nature have their minds set on what that nature desires; but those who live in accordance with the Spirit have their minds set on what the Spirit desires. The mind of sinful man is death, but the mind controlled by the Spirit is life and peace; the sinful mind is hostile to God" (Rom. 8:5–7).

Now there exists a new resurgence of interest in the supernatural as seen in the growing New Age movement and increasing cult activity. The recognition that reality transcends the tangible and encompasses the supernatural has generated a renewed search to know and experience God. This search by secular society for an understanding of God is peaking in every part of the world, including the atheistic former Soviet Union.

William Buckley has spoken of a quickly passing era. The academy he attended considered God-talk irrelevant. He explained, "God was not only banished, but was an embarrassment to the sophisticate." He spoke of the reluctance of these sophisticates to invite a colleague to dinner a second time if he mentioned God or religion during a previous social gathering.[3]

I believed at one time that unbelieving society was by nature hostile to God. It meant that anyone I spoke to about Christ would be hostile. I lived in fear of ever speaking to anyone about Christ because I anticipated their hostility. Is that your experience?

Somehow we have taken the verses in the Word that speak of persecution of believers in the name of Christ and distorted them to teach that everyone we meet is a probable Christian-basher. We feed into the devil's plan to silence us. Our fears may be one of the major reasons secular society remains ignorant about the Christian faith.

James Wall made a very interesting observation in his article "God as a Hobby." He wrote, "We live in a culture of disbelief not because the media of nonbelievers want it that way, but because those who claim to be religious are afraid someone will say they sound 'like Bakker or Swaggart', televangelists previously discredited." [4]

Rather than the overt hostility we've been led to believe surrounds us, it appears that much of the resistance from the secular community flows from fear of the unknown. American journalists are certainly expressing this opinion. "We're trained to be doubters, cynics and skeptics," *USA Today* journalist John Seigenthaler confessed at a national forum at Columbia University. "Perhaps that's why we're so comfortable with politicians." [5] The fact that "hard news" is grounded in facts, whereas religious news presumes a faith beyond the facts which is unfamiliar to them, accounts for the reason many journalists would rather write about almost anything else.

U.S. News and World Report reported, "Few newsrooms are equipped to take religion seriously." [6] Unbelievers don't want to appear stupid any more than anyone else.

So if society's primary resistance to our message is a result of discomfort with the intangible and fear of the unknown, how can you and I think biblically and reach out to those we meet each day? First, as we discussed in chapter 3, we can overcome our own fears. This ability, coupled with sensitivity, gentleness, and genuine concern for the individual provides opportunities for investing our lives in the things that really matter—in the lives of individuals we meet who are without hope.

Jesus always dealt with the individual. He did not come to earth to change the world system, government, or masses. He could have easily done so in less than a moment. Jesus came to touch and transform individuals. The secular society is simply a multitude of individuals who need a touch from the Savior.

Where can we start? In our homes. Do you have a prodigal child, an unbelieving spouse, or resistant relative? How can you begin to see that family member through the eyes of God? He loves them more than you ever could. In the Word you learn how God reaches out to those He loves.

Marian Wright Edelman, president of the Children's Defense Fund, wrote, "Despite social tidal waves, I believe there are some enduring spiritual and national values that we need to rediscover . . . It is the responsibility of every adult—parent, teacher, preacher, and professional—to make sure that children and young people hear what we have learned from life, learn what we think matters, and know that they are never alone as they go to seize the future. So I have written my three wonderful sons a long letter sharing twenty-five of the lessons life has taught me."[7]

Take a moment to read the good news in the Gospels. See Jesus, the Lord of the universe, as He walks through His own world. See the faces He sees, touch the people He touches, hear the cries of nature and calls of needy, lonely men and women—the sounds He hears. Imagine the paths He often walked, taste the dust in your mouth as the wind whips around you, smell the spray of lake water as it laps the boat's rim while he teaches. Meet Jesus, then introduce those around you to the one who loves you and them individually.

Have you ever thought of doing that? I am ashamed to admit I hadn't. How do we communicate the deepest beliefs of our souls with not only our family, but with friends, and the larger society in which we live? We get involved in their lives, and through doing so we invest our lives in things that matter.

Deb Zgraggen found a way to do this. A former insurance claims adjuster and mother of two in Ravena, New York, she was concerned about the lack of academic challenge for her high-achieving six-year-old. When she learned that children did not become eligible for the district's gifted and talented program until third grade, Zgraggen assembled her forces.

She pulled out the class list she'd kept from a kindergarten party the year before, contacted the PTA president and called other parents she'd met at school functions. They formed a group and held meetings. They invited speakers and gave their group an important-sounding name.

Eventually, after influencing the right people, Zgraggen managed to spearhead a revamped gifted program. Her mission was accomplished.[8]

Was Deb a threat? Did she set out with a chip on her shoulder, sure that the secular public school system would resist and resent her intrusion? No. She showed her child, his educators, and other parents how much she cared. She was willing to get involved. If an individual can create change in an educational situation, certainly the Christian can do the same in a non-Christian world.

Sometimes because of the presuppositions about the secular world instilled in our thinking by Christian leadership, we set out to make a difference as if we're ready for a fight. This certainly is not Jesus' approach when dealing with unbelievers. We need to realize that we can make a significant difference in our world as we touch the lives of individuals.

Lynda Beams of Fort Worth demonstrates this truth. When flipping on the "Geraldo" show one afternoon, Lynda was amazed to hear guests asked if they had sex with animals. "A chill ran down my spine. Children home from school could be watching this." Deeply concerned, she switched off the TV and began a crusade to remove TV talk shows from after-school time slots.

"I'd sensed God directing me to get involved in cleaning up the airwaves, but I was nervous," she explains. "I'm not an activist by nature. I'm shy, soft-spoken and have been raising my children for twenty years. I didn't know where to begin."

But begin she did, and God supplied the direction. Starting with a simple petition asking the TV stations to monitor the programs, she then taped six shows, creating a fifteen-minute videotape to send to Geraldo's national and local sponsors. She wanted to impress them with the kind of programming their money was buying.

Every sponsor canceled their sponsorship. Finally after 19 months, a petition with 14,000 signatures, 107 sponsor withdrawals, 700 protest letters to the network, and a statewide PTA resolution protesting the time slot, the local TV station removed the program from the Dallas/Fort Worth viewing area.

When asked what she learned through this experience and others she has pursued since, she remarks, "I've learned over the last four years that it's not the one with the most money, the biggest audience or the most power who wins, it's the one with the most perseverance. I'm convinced that if God would raise up ten women around the country who share my passion and concern about these issues, we would get the entertainment industry cleaned up by the year 2000."[9]

Lynda cared. Her concern was not for issues but people, and God honored her desire to be used by Him to make a difference.

Who are you concerned about right now? Your child? Your spouse? Your neighbor or friend? You can make a difference. You can invest in things that matter. God will give you the ability to touch a life for His glory as you respond with gentleness and genuine concern.

———————

PART FOUR

Captivating
the World
for Christ

Are you a winsome person? Do you want to be? How can you effectively reach secular society with the message of Jesus Christ? Investing your life in the only things with eternal value, God's Word and the people who join you in the heaven-bound journey, makes investing yourself in the world a challenge you don't want to miss.

How do you accomplish the task? What are the principles? Is it a matter of taking the world captive, cornering them mercilessly, and insisting on their compliance as you shove God's truth down their throats? Or is it a matter of presenting the person of Jesus in such a way that they are captivated by His love, drawn by His caring, and intrigued by His truth?

In this section, aspects of the culture in which you live will be highlighted. Fresh insights and new understanding of the secular society in which God has placed you will be presented. You will learn from the life experiences of others creative ways to captivate the world for Christ. Individuals who are making significant strides investing their lives in things that matter will be spotlighted.

Evaluate and consider new opportunities for your life investments as you appreciate the investments of others for Christ's sake.

CHAPTER FOURTEEN

UNDERSTANDING YOUR NEIGHBOR AND YOUR WORLD

Have you desired to touch lives for eternity but you don't know how? You feel inadequate and unprepared. Making investments without proper information is tough, but the Holy Spirit promises to be our teacher. He will equip each of us if we ask.

But you will receive power when the Holy Spirit comes on you; and you will be my witnesses.

ACTS 1:8

*J*anet's face reflected pain and stress too deep to verbalize. Gray-blue eyes stared blankly. Shoulder length, gray-streaked hair may not have been touched by a brush that day. Her skin, leathered by the sun, creased and folded with wrinkles, looked like the face of an old woman. Janet was in her forties, much too young to look so old. The smell of stale coffee permeated her breath as she spoke.

"I never see my husband. His patients demand all of his time. I stay alone with the two kids most of the time. I guess we make out all right.

"Actually, I'm pretty depressed. Toys, sterile walls, carpooling, and dishes just aren't my thing. Robert says I need a hobby. So I've taken up painting. It's OK. I just can't seem to get into it. I took a self-actualization course at the community college last semester. Didn't help much.

"I've been trying to figure out what I'm about ever since the sixties. Robert and I were at Woodstock. We met as hippies. He's become a doctor and I haven't become, period." A weary, sad chuckle barely escaped her lips. "There's got to be more than this," she sighs until there seems no breath left in her body.

I asked her if she had any interest in God.

"Oh, religion? We've started going to the Universalist, Unitarian church. After the kids were born we figured we better go somewhere. We didn't go to church for years because Robert and I were living together before we got married. We were both raised Catholic. We knew the church wouldn't approve so we just didn't go. Neither of us were ever very religious anyway."

Have you seen anyone lately like Janet? An individual wandering, lost through the secular world. Most know only the strains of the secular ballad—an eerie and seductive melody demanding their allegiance, capturing their souls. They are not as convinced of its message as they appear. They simply know its tune.

What is its tune? Have you heard it? Have you listened to its nuances? The secular philosophy of our culture today is both fascinating and devastating. The people captured by it are to be pitied and loved rather than contemptuously scorned. Few are hostile; most are entranced.

How can you make a difference? Listening is the first step. If you are secure in your faith, you won't feel threatened by the thoughts and ideas of the world. You can listen with compassion. In fact you may be challenged, caused to think. But you always know that you have a secure and unchanging guide by which to compare your thoughts—the truth of God's Word.

God's Word will never change. It will never disappoint you. As long as your beliefs rest there, they cannot be threatened. And any beliefs that are not consistent with the truth of God's Word need to be questioned and eliminated anyway.

This assurance and security in God and His Word frees you to listen attentively, to be more concerned for the individual than for protecting or defending your faith. Secure in God, you can listen beyond the secular ballad and hear the strains of a heart searching for life's purpose—searching for God.

Paul did exactly this as he walked within the culture where God had placed him. He evaluated the society and responded to the dilemma of their souls. In Acts, Paul identifies the aimless wandering: "For as I walked around and looked carefully at your objects of worship, I even found an altar with this inscription: to an unknown god"(Acts 17:23). Paul recognized their groping, their desire to be sure all their options were covered. They weren't sure who God was or if there was just one God. They simply hoped that in their wandering they had appeased him.

Paul quotes the poets of the day, "As some of your own poets have said, 'We are his offspring'" (Acts 17:28). Paul was aware of their culture. He had read their poets and knew of their teachers. He had been willing to listen. And out of that which they did know, he could point to the one they didn't know—the God of the universe they so needed.

Are we like Paul, attentively observing our culture and discovering new methods to communicate the living gospel to a dying world? Take the following quiz to see how much you are in touch with the ideas and needs of your world.

In Touch with Contemporary Society

1. How often do you read the local newspaper?
2. What is a best-selling book on the secular market today?
3. What time is national news offered on your television?
4. What year does the next presidential election take place?
5. When was the last time you read a secular novel?
6. List three issues of national concern.
7. List three issues of world concern and explain their implications for our country.
8. What news magazine do you subscribe to?
9. When was the last time you had a conversation with anyone about an issue concerning our nation?
10. Describe your last conversation with an unbeliever. What were the needs you identified in his or her life?

If you just realized you aren't really in touch with society, my intention is not to cause you guilt or bring condemnation. My intention is to enable you to consider new ways to profitably invest your life. Understand your culture so you can begin to understand the people in it. Build relationships and talk with people. Use events, facts, experiences, and information they know and understand in the same way Paul used the words of the poets and teachers of his day, to lead to discussions of Jesus and His life and words.

Listening in a way that builds relationships prepares you to invest your life and biblically consistent beliefs in the lives of others.

Bob Dowd who works for ARM (Associates Resourcing Missions) voices his concerns,

> I am most concerned about relationships because relationship is the primary purpose for which we are created. God created us in His image to have relationship with Him and to have relationship with others around us.
>
> So often I see in my sphere of influence (business and government) that people are basing their identity in their function (what they do, job, etc.) and not who they are. Relationships are the crux of the hope for our future, for out of proper relationships values are formed and transferred, evangelism is naturally produced, and major issues of the day can be put in perspective.
>
> I would envision a time of understanding why we believe what we believe and why others hold their beliefs through their world view.

When I travel and speak, I often introduce one of my seminars by holding up a greeting card that shows city streets teeming with cars followed by the text, "In this busy high-tech world, if you are ever in need of some personal human contact, just call me . . . and leave a message after the beep." This one card demonstrates the poverty of relationships in our culture.

Chuck Colson wrote, "The tie that binds us as a nation is no longer common belief or heritage. The closest we come to a shared experience of common language are the messages and mores that flow out of our television sets. So phrases like 'Where's the Beef?' and the adventures of Wayne's World . . . are our common bonds of communication within American culture."[1]

The following steps will enable you to invest your life in people and in things that matter.

1. Familiarize yourself with the events and thinking of the culture.
2. Ask the Holy Spirit for sensitivity toward those He brings across your path. Make time in your schedule for God's sovereign intervention. Prepare to spend time with others as opportunity arises and He directs.

3. Associate with unbelievers without fear. Pray for opportunities to meet with and build relationships with those who are searching for Christ.
4. Be genuine in building relationships. Don't see every unbeliever as a mission project. See each as a person with genuine needs, concerns, sorrows, and joys that you can appreciate and from whom you can learn. Care about them. Jesus didn't merely tolerate the multitudes as statistics for evangelism. Jesus looked upon and cared for the multitudes with compassion.
5. Build trust in the relationship. Let persons see your genuine concern for their well-being and interest in their lives.
6. Listen carefully to the concerns and interests being shared. Use the information you accumulate concerning secular society to provide a bridge of mutual understanding for conversation.
7. Share your faith naturally by simply sharing what the Lord has done for you. The earliest disciples modeled this form of evangelism. They simply told what the Lord had done for them. John begins his first letter, "That which was from the beginning, which we have heard, which we have seen with our eyes, which we have looked at and our hands have touched—this we proclaim concerning the Word of life" (1 John 1:1).
8. Commit yourself for the duration. Be willing to get involved and remain involved as your relationship with each individual develops. Always remember that you represent Christ in your behavior and attitude.

I received several interesting comments after I led a seminar on relationships. Christina Shoemaker wrote, "Christian relationships in society are fundamental. So much mission work focuses on leaving one's own society to reach untouched people. There are many lost people right in my own backyard—this is my mission."

Another woman wrote, "Christian relationships in society, in the workplace, concern me. We shrink from dealing with the world. We isolate ourselves. How will the world be drawn to the Savior?

Many are concerned about world missions, but our outreach must begin next door, on the job, etc."

Who Are These People?

Who will you meet if you choose to step outside the Christian community and touch the world? You will meet people just like you. You will meet people who are troubled and hurting, looking for answers. You will meet people who are complacent and hard to reach. The difference between you and them is that you have the answer, Jesus Christ, the Truth.

These statistics from the May 1993 *Clarion-Ledger* in Jackson, Mississippi, tell a story in themselves.

Every 60 minutes in America:

+ 125 young people see their parents divorce
+ 107 children are born out of wedlock
+ 137 children run away from home
+ 77 children are abused and/or neglected
+ 66 teenagers drop out of school
+ 117 teens (women under 20) get pregnant
+ 323 teenagers are sexually active
+ 46 teenagers have abortions
+ 1 teenager commits suicide.
+ Finally, less than 60 percent of all children today are living with biological, married parents.

These represent the needy all around you as well. You, too, may be found in one of these statistics. What can you share? Paul explains your message clearly,

> All praise to the God and Father of our Master, Jesus the Messiah! Father of all mercy! God of all healing counsel! He comes alongside us when we go through hard times, and before you know it, he brings us alongside someone else who is going through hard times so that we can be there for that person just as God was there for us. We have plenty of hard times that come

from following the Messiah, but no more so than the good times of his healing comfort—we get a full measure of that, too.

2 CORINTHIANS 1:4–6, THE MESSAGE

Communicating the Gospel Clearly

As relationships build, as caring occurs and genuine concern begins, opportunities will arise for communicating faith. How can you express your faith clearly? At one time the phrase "The Bible says . . ." commanded immediate respect. But today it is said that only 32 percent believe the Bible is true.

Because most of the culture adamantly rejects the idea of absolutes, it becomes easy for anyone to dismiss another's personal testimony. When a Christian speaks of the truth of Christianity and the Bible, the response may be, "Well, that's fine for you—that's your point of view, but I have another standard." Or perhaps, "My New Age friend has found peace in her life through her belief as well." It's easy to be silenced.

Chuck Colson tells of his experience giving his testimony to a prominent journalist. After attempting all the usual angles, when rebuffed, Colson caught the journalist off guard.

> I asked, "Have you seen Woody Allen's *Crimes and Misdemeanors*? 'Are you Judah Rosenthal?'"
>
> He laughed, but it was a nervous laugh.
>
> "You may think this life is all there is," I said, "but if so, there is still an issue at hand—how do you live with yourself while you're here? I know you have a conscience. So how do you deal with that when you know you do wrong?"
>
> He picked at his food and told me that that very issue had caused him a lot of problems. Then we somehow moved into a discussion of Leo Tolstoy's novel *War and Peace*, in which Pierre, the central character, cries out, *"Why is it that I know what is right but do what is wrong?"* That in turn led us to C. S. Lewis's concept of the natural law ingrained in all of us, and then to the central point of Romans 1: that we all are imbued with a conscience, run from it, though we might, and that conscience itself points to questions which can only be answered outside of ourselves.
>
> I don't know what's going to happen to my friend. My hunch is he's going to come to Christ, because I believe the Holy Spirit

is hounding him . . . And I know another thing: without Woody Allen, Leo Tolstoy, and C. S. Lewis, we wouldn't have had a common ground and language with which to discuss the spiritual realm.[2]

You don't need to be an intellectual to reach others for Christ, but you do need to be aware of the culture in which God has placed you and the needs and concerns of those you meet. As you seek to invest your life in the people God brings across your path, His Holy Spirit will give you the resources you need to meet every situation. But remember, the responsibility for salvation is not yours, it's God's.

My dear friend and concert musician, Teresa Moshell, told me several weeks ago, "God has brought me to a new place in my ministry. I realize now that I am not God's sole resource for touching people's lives. My role may be to simply plant the seed of the gospel, water it along the way to maturity, or have the privilege of being involved in the harvest. I will be content to be used by Him in whatever way He desires. I really understand the verse, 'What after all is Apollos? And what is Paul? Only servants, through whom you came to believe—as the Lord has assigned to each His task. I planted the seed, Apollos watered it, but God made it grow'(1 Cor. 3:5–6). I'm just grateful to be His servant."

As you reach out and begin to invest your life in people, realize that though it takes time and commitment to get involved and to care, nothing will reap greater rewards or produce higher dividends. In the following chapters we'll look at some issues that face our culture, discuss the biblical truth involved, and describe what others have done to meet the challenge.

Anyone can make a difference. It's really not difficult. It simply requires a heart in love with Jesus and a desire to do His will. Are you ready?

WHO CARES ABOUT ISSUES AND WHY?

What do today's issues have to do with investing your life in things that matter? Are they fads to be ignored or avenues of opportunity? Learn more about evaluating and responding to contemporary issues that may have seemed meaningless before.

The LORD God took the man and put him in the Garden of Eden to work it and take care of it.

GENESIS 2:15

*T*he environment? Sure, it's important. But who has time to think about it?" my friend blurted. Her exasperation and impatience were apparent.

Her brows were drawn and tense. "Linda, I've got three kids, clothes to wash, a house to clean, carpool to run . . . Do you think I have time to save three garbage cans in my house? One for cans, one for glass, and one for who knows what? And then to collect them and take them to *another* garbage area all the way across town? Are you kidding? Get real."

She had a point. The office staff had just begun recycling, and I was trying to decide how I felt about it. It did seem like a *lot* of trouble, and for what? *Another secular fad that will fade like tie-dyed T-shirts and leather thongs,* I thought.

"I get so mad," she continued. "I'm sick and tired of everybody telling me what I should do or must do to be a spiritual Christian. Is *garbage* a standard for spirituality now? What next? I have had it."

I quickly changed the subject, but her hostility was unmistakable. Was she right? What did the garbage have to do with Christianity, and was it something worth caring about?

Though I didn't bring it up again with my friend, I began collecting information about the environmental issue. The secular culture had to have a reason for the new focus, and at the same time I wanted to know what God thought about it. Did it deserve a Christian response, or was it simply another phase to be ignored? I always try to collect and evaluate information before I take a stand. I seldom jump on bandwagons, so my investigation began.

The Contemporary Perspective

For the first time, I noticed articles that dealt with the environment. No longer passive, my interest peaked as I learned more about the religious beliefs undergirding this movement.

I soon discovered that the secular, environmentalist issue was in reality a spiritual one. It is fast developing into a theology. The worship of "Mother Earth" has taken a new twist. Searching for spiritual answers, an increasing number of environmentalists have turned to the earth goddess Gaia, scientific theory, and a New Age icon. "Gaia is the New Age darling of spiritual feminists, neo-pagans, political environmentalists and animal rights activists" wrote Tod Conner in his article, "Is the Earth Alive?"

Unsure whether Gaia promoters consider it science or religion, he wrote, "In the past three years, more than 100 scientific and technical articles have been written on the Gaia theory." Gaia was introduced twenty years ago by James Lovelock, an atmospheric scientist, inventor, and respected member of Britain's elite Royal Society. Lovelock extolled his scientific concept of a living earth which he thought of calling "the Biocybernic Universal System Tendency/Homeostasis." At the suggestion of author William Golding, who wrote the best-selling book, *Lord of the Flies*, Lovelock changed the name to "Gaia."[1]

That didn't sound good at all, but the information got worse. Lynn Margulis, internationally known professor of microbiology at the University of Massachusetts, has endorsed this theory, thereby giving it respectability because of her personal credentials. Her most recent book "traces" the evolution of life from its original "bacterial ooze."

Later, I learned more about Gaia. Rowena Pattie Kryder of the California Institute of Integral Studies in San Francisco, going a step further, developed an elaborate "scientific" theory based on the "language" of Gaia . . . "how Gaia 'talks to herself' and to us, her children. If we are "addicted, confused, and express disempowering tendencies, Gaia reacts with earthquakes, tornadoes, floods and extreme weather changes that force us to reassess our values, work together, and create a way of life anew."[2]

Further, whenever "'some living entity' becomes enlightened about its true nature and its relationship to other living things, Gaia is happy and experiences intrinsic joy herself."[3]

So it becomes clear that this is not some passive issue about depositing our garbage in designated areas. It's an issue of spiritual implication, and as a Christian I realized it was important for me to decide what I believed.

Insights on the religious underpinnings of this movement proved interesting. What was the thrust of the secular philosophy? That was my next pursuit. I started asking questions of Christians who I felt were "in the know." One key individual was Norm Bomer, editor of *God's World* magazine, a weekly news reader for kids written from a Christian perspective. I was not disappointed. Norm offered a wealth of information that was both startling and fascinating.

Norm explained that modern environmentalists view the corruption of our environment as man's failure, more specifically the failure of the Judeo-Christian theological position. That surprised me. It's interesting that Christians "take the rap" for the world's mistakes.

Norm went on to say that many environmentalists believe that by elevating ourselves as image-bearers of God, we are violating the sacredness of "Mother Earth." They also believe the earth could and would have the freedom to return to its pristine perfection. This means the end of man's interference with it. The repercussions of man's sin, "the fall," and the curse are nonexistent in their opinion.

I guess they haven't visited my garden plot since I stopped planting. Fallen creation only produces thistles and weeds when left untended. I think they missed that point.

As Christians we understand the earth's plight is due to man's sin. "Cursed is the ground because of you; through painful toil you will eat of it all the days of your life. It will produce thorns and thistles for you" (Gen. 3:17–18). Such is the end of untamed and uncared for land. Animals destroy each other and weeds overtake the neglected landscape. The removal of man will not provide a solution or change this reality.

The facts would be alarming except for the knowledge that God is in charge and is managing everything. I think some of the quotes of environmental activists will amaze you:

+ In 1967, Lynn White, medieval historian and environmental activist, called Christianity, "the most anthropocentric [man-centered] religion the world has ever seen and claimed that through such ideas as human dominion, the desacralization of nature [refusing to announce nature as sacred], and the belief that ultimate human destiny is with God [not the Earth] Christendom has encouraged a destructive use of creation."[4]

+ Catholic theologian Matthew Fox says, "We should turn from a theology centered on sin and redemption and develop a creation spirituality, with nature as our primary revelation and sin a distant memory."[5]

+ The founder of Friends of the Earth has been quoted as saying, "The death of a young man in war is no more tragic than the touching of mountains and wilderness areas by man."[6]

+ One main platform of the Sierra Club, as defined in its constitution, is to promote worldwide abortion to save the earth from people, Norm continues. Statements in the Sierra Club Charter read, "The Sierra Club urges that each of the individual states of the United States legalize abortion . . . Increased population density creates environmental problems . . . regulation of population growth within nations is a proper subject for policy formation and other action by the United States. . . . to control regulation by the availability of information and facilities, where needed, for the whole range of reproductive control . . . The continued enjoyment of natural areas without irreparably impairing those areas depends on formulation of careful policies for population reduction and proper land use."[7]

As Norm and I closed our visit, he left me with these thoughts. "So much of what the environmentalists say may sound good, but it poses a genuine threat to the free-enterprise system, our life, our world, not to mention the Christian community.

"Environmentalists want to get rid of the problem and its source—mankind. It is a selfish, narcissistic view. Rather than subduing, using, and developing the earth, the environmentalists who are fanatic want to put it on a shelf and worship it."

Following my conversation with Norm, I decided to gather information to clarify my concerns. What were some positive results of the movement's efforts? Statistics proved most helpful. In the May 1995 issue of *Smithsonian*, Jimmy Anderson, nurseryman for Georgia Pacific, reported that his company was growing 50 million seedlings a year now to take care of the trees, attempting to offset forest depletion.

Philips Petroleum recycles 100 million plastic bottles yearly so that "land fills will be filled with other things like land," reducing land waste and conserving natural resources. The Chemical Manufacturers Association captured over a billion pounds of toxic chemical waste and converted it to energy. "It's not the whole answer, but it's a start," the association announced.[8]

The simple facts herald the truth that God's creation, our world, benefits from the interest and activity of those who have chosen to get involved. Plant and animal life have been preserved. This in turn creates a healthier environment for all of us.

But there is more. In this book we have discussed foundations for biblical thinking. As Christians it is our responsibility not only to gather information about the religious and philosophical implications of an issue, observe the positive outcome of actions taken, but also to form a biblical world and life view. Sharp biblical thinking enables us to form a belief, act upon it, and communicate its truth to each other. Creating this personal belief about the environment was my next step.

I wanted to understand God's position concerning the environment. How would a biblical philosophy toward the environment compare to the issues mentioned earlier? I found in Scripture the foundational principles for the Christian. We are first described as God's "image-bearers."

"Let us make man in our image, in our likeness, and let them rule over the fish of the sea and the birds of the air, over the livestock, over all the earth, and over all the creatures that move along the ground"(Gen. 1:26).

You and I are distinctly different from all other living things because we are "stamped" with God's image. In all of creation, we alone bear His likeness. In addition, we have been given a task—to rule over, subdue, use, develop, and steward the rest of creation responsibly. It is given to us for our survival as well as its preservation.

I knew that this was a responsible Christian position, one I personally had overlooked. Appreciating God's creation and growing a garden to provide fresh vegetables for my family never posed a problem. Caring for the garden hadn't really been a personal priority. Like my friend who introduced the chapter, life presented too many demands and stresses to attend to my "creation" responsibilities.

Calvin B. DeWitt in his article, "Myth #2: It's Not Biblical to be Green," describes childhood experiences of appreciating God's creation. From caring for a turtle in a tank as a three-year-old to caring for a backyard zoo in his youth, he considered all creatures God's masterpieces.

> As a youth I savored Article II of the Reformed tradition's Belgic Confession. In answering "By What Means Is God Made Known to Us?" the first part affirms, "by the creation, preservation, and government of the universe; which is before our eyes as a most elegant book, wherein all creatures, great and small, are as so many characters leading us to see clearly the invisible things of God."
>
> This theme of how creation tells of God's glory and love is echoed throughout Scripture; God lovingly provides the rain and cyclings of water, provides food for creatures, fills people's hearts with joy, and satisfies the earth (Ps. 104:10–18; Acts 14:17). It is through this manifest love and wisdom that creation declares God's glory and proclaims the work of the Creator's hands (Ps. 19:1). Creation gives clear evidence of God's eternal power and divinity, leaving everyone without excuse before God (Rom. 1:20).[9]

To "subdue the earth" as translated in the King James Version of Scripture, does not refer to abusing and destroying. It refers to tending and caring for in a way that nurtures both creation and mankind. Loren Wilkinson in the article, "Myth #3: There Is Nothing Christians Can Do," gives clear direction for Christian responsibility in creation care.

> We need to practice the principles of "reduce, reuse, recycle"—not out of environmentalist legalism but in conscious delight of being God's free, redeemed, and responsible stewards:
> We *reduce*, for example, because, though creation is for our use, it has worth far beyond the use we make of it.
> We *reuse*, because God did not make a throw-away world.
> And we *recycle* because God does. "To the place the streams come from, there they return again," says Psalm 104.

She adds that we in our culture need to resist the consumerism we find in television and in advertising and refuse to be shaped by them. The positive result: joy. We rejoice in God's provision for the earth. "Isaiah's words should describe our experience of creation, . . . 'You will go out in joy and be led forth in peace; the mountains and hills will burst into song before you, and all the trees of the field will clap their hands'" (Isa. 55:12).[10]

I tried to compare this creational view of the environment to the secular philosophy. So is this a passive issue to be ignored? I don't think so. Am I afraid of the anti-Christian implications? No. Jesus already told me, "In this world you will have trouble. But take heart! I have overcome the world" (John 16:33). Have I started separating my garbage? Yes, actually. Most of the time. I have decided in response to God's creation mandate in Genesis, we as Christians should have been at the forefront of this issue desiring to care for the creation God has given us. But since we weren't, we can join in to make a difference in both the movement and its philosophy. Calvin DeWitt closes his article with the excellent statement,

> The evangelical community has been slow to get involved in environmental issues. But it is not too late. In the early 1970's there were few evangelicals involved in world hunger. Today some of the best relief operations are done by these deliberative evangelicals. They did not just start handing out food. They got the best minds together, collected the scriptural material, and carefully planned.

This needs to happen again. Our environmental situation presents a significant opportunity. To be *evangelical* means to proclaim the good news. Part of our proclamation is that the environment is God's creation. If we do not make God the Creator part of the Good News, we are crippling our faith and witness.[11]

Why have I taken so much time on this issue? Because I hope it helps you consider how to apply everything we've discussed in this book. What principles can we apply when deciding what we believe about any issue presently consuming the interest of our culture?

LOOKING AT THE ISSUES

1. Don't react. Act only after personal consideration of the issue.
2. Gather the facts. What can you learn about the issue both from secular media and from informed Christians? If you don't have friends who are up on the subject, go to your local Christian bookstore and look for periodicals or books that address the issue. Call your local Christian radio station and get telephone numbers of ministries that are familiar with the issue in question.
3. Ask God for His perspective. What is His position on the issue? Turn to the Bible for answers. Pray the Holy Spirit will lead to truth on the subject.
4. Avoid becoming unnecessarily fearful. Don't cloud the issue. Make an informed and biblically accurate evaluation.
5. Decide what you personally believe; remain teachable and open to new insights from God's Word.
6. Act on your belief.

How are Christian people responding to these cultural concerns in a way that reflects Christ? Meet Ruth Brinker. She addressed the environmental issue and that of the hungry and homeless at the same time. Here's Ruth's story.

Americans know that the world's population increases with each passing year. They also know that land to produce the food for this burgeoning growth decreases annually. Suburb development around cities, poor ecological practices and decreased land areas contribute to the problem.

Ruth thinks she may have the answer for the inner-city dweller. Roofs. Roofs topped with gardens. Where did the idea come from?

Ruth and a couple of women basked in the California sun on a warm summer day. They chatted about the world's problems. "We were sitting together, shucking Louisiana butterbeans when someone said, 'Wouldn't it be nice if the homeless could enjoy something like his?' and I thought, *Why not?* And that was the first step in my determination to teach people bio-intensive farming."

Not satisfied to sit back, dream and spend her time regretting that she could do little as an individual, Ruth went into action to make her dream come true. The idea for rooftop farming came to her when a friend, who had an art school next to the city's biggest homeless shelter, invited her to an advisory board meeting. "My friend is on the advisory board. I came up with the idea, so the meeting ended with everyone being very enthusiastic about the rooftop farming idea. We discovered that most buildings can't support this type of farming, but there are rooftops on industrial buildings which are usually OK. With the rooftop farm, the homeless families housed in the building's studio apartments can simply go upstairs and go to work."

The difficult job of finding land began. She contacted a group of developers who buy industrial buildings off the market to convert to low-income housing. Together they are planning to place a farm on one of the buildings within the year.

Over the years, Ruth has never given up her dream of helping both the homeless become more self-sufficient and also do something constructive about the environment.

"My plan is to grow a lot of produce in the city on the rooftops which will also be good for the environment. Plants absorb carbon dioxide and provide us with oxygen. Also food won't have to be trucked fifty or seventy-five miles because we don't have land to grow too many things in the city.

"We'll be giving people the freshest produce they've ever had in their lives. I'm training homeless people in bio-intensive organic farming and hope to create a number of urban farms."

Dozens of restaurants in the city have promised to buy the organically grown food that is now being planted in Brinker's quarter-acre demonstration farm on the corner of Ellis and Davisadero Streets. Fresh Start Farms teaches the homeless how to grow the exotic vegetables and edible flowers in demand in San Francisco eateries.

"We hope to gross $100,000 in our first year. My plan is to get all the people involved in this program off of welfare in a year. We'll start small and work from there, but I think we'll be successful.

"A lot of people don't realize that a good percentage of the homeless are just like anyone else. They aren't derelicts, but working people who are trying to get off the streets. I'd like to help them turn their lives around.[12]

Ruth's story is one of many. Many Christians are beginning to see the opportunities the environmental issue offers. An international evangelical forum held a conference in Washington, D.C., recently, choosing the topic "Evangelical Christianity and the Environment" as one way to look at the Christian approach to caring for the planet and planning strategies for the future.

Theologians, scholars, youth workers, a forest ranger and high-ranking government officials from the U.S. and Great Britain concluded that the secular environmental movement reveals a deep spiritual hunger that evangelicals can respond to—if they take a fresh look at the Bible.

"If churches fail to embrace a theology of care for the creation, they will lose today's youth who have gone from fear of the bomb to that of an ecological doomsday," declared one youth worker. The forum participants predicted that more evangelicals will begin to develop environmental sensitivities.[13]

Joe Ebenezer, member of the Christian environmental organization Green Cross, says, "When Christians make sacrifices on behalf of others, or take personal health risks in a cleanup, people are bound to discover at some point that love of Christ and Creation are the motivating factors."[14]

These people have demonstrated that when you take interest in the culture and decide what you believe, you can invest in things that matter by taking actions that testify to the faith that motivates you.

CHAPTER SIXTEEN

BRUSHSTROKES
ON THE CANVAS OF LIFE

Have you thought of doing what you love to do
while making a statement to the world?
Do you like music, drama, or writing?
What does the Bible say about the arts,
a field that is rocking our world?

So whether you eat or drink or whatever you do, do it all for the glory of God.

1 CORINTHIANS 10:31

Ken Myers sits amidst blue foam-layered walls and ceiling—a silent catacomb for his work. From his console in the center with a microphone suspended from above, Ken speaks with authority about news, art, history, science, technology, all the elements that comprise "culture." Ken is a culture analyst. And Ken has a mission. He produces audiocassette tapes that inform the Christian community of cultural change and diversity.

"I feel it's essential that we as Christians understand our culture as well as the secular world. Our analysis of cultural affairs needs to be as intelligent and well-informed as theirs.

"With this in mind, I established a sound studio in the two-car garage behind my house, now expanded to include a five-room building including a 10,000-volume library. In it I write, direct and produce a bimonthly audio magazine of contemporary culture and Christian conviction."

What gives Ken the expertise to do this? Executive editor of *Eternity*, an evangelical monthly magazine, and former producer/editor for National Public Radio's two news programs, "Morning Edition" and "All Things Considered," Ken's knowledge and experience thoroughly equip him for the task.

"Cultural apologetics is my field. Throughout my work, I want to emphasize the importance of evangelism, the need to walk daily with the Lord, to study God's Word, to live a life of prayer, and show love, compassion, and the holiness of our Lord while emphasizing equally the need to live this out in every area of culture and society.

"My conviction," he says, "is that orthodoxy and cultural alertness are not necessarily antagonists. Viewing the world with critical intelligence and wit is a natural part of glorifying and enjoying God.

"Many Christians only think about the contours of modern culture when a moral crisis erupts in their personal lives: a daughter has an abortion, a son is addicted to cocaine, a neighbor leaves his family and job to join a pantheistic cult. But the day-to-day challenges of living with an increasingly corrosive culture are rarely addressed. Understanding culture means staying well-informed about specific cultural activities (e.g., books, films, fads, etc.), while developing a feel for the larger patterns of culture."

Ken exemplifies this truth with excellence. And one way he does this is to acknowledge, evaluate, and provide a biblical understanding of the arts. He regularly updates his listeners as to current trends in the arts and issues that affect the Christian.

Unfortunately, few Christians feel comfortable with the arts. The arts may conjure ideas of nude paintings and sensual theater performances. The reality is that although all of these are freely found on the television every day, few of us eliminate television from our lives. Why are the arts banned?

What are your thoughts about the arts? Have you, too, avoided the issue or treated professional artists like lepers? I pose the questions because the fields of art desperately need God's ordained touch of Christian creativity.

As you choose to invest your life in things that matter I would challenge you to reconsider fields of interest you may have previously shunned. So many who make these fields their life are spiritually destitute. They are rarely touched or spoken to by a believing Christian. Their hearts are as hungry as any other unbeliever. Why should they be denied the message of the gospel?

Take a moment to review the response principles in chapter 15. Those same principles apply to evaluating our response to our involvement in the arts.

Carol Bomer is one woman who acts daily on her beliefs. Carol is making an impact in the challenging field of art. Her art becomes the means by which her Christian testimony is proclaimed.

"Paint is the medium God has given me to proclaim His truth to the secular world," Carol explains. "My constant pursuit is to make the Scriptures real in paint. My desire is to integrate in paint, spirit and flesh, both reality and non-reality, the truth that Jesus Christ is the God-man."

The brochure for Carol's recent exhibit, titled "The Unveiling," quotes her, "The spiritual world can be painted by both non-objective abstraction and objective realism. Through Christ, who is both God and man, Spirit and flesh, this seeming dichotomy is resolved. In my work I attempt to join the tangible world and the spiritual world apprehended through the eyes of faith."

"Spiritual" painting, a current art trend, supplies Carol with numerous opportunities to display her work in the secular arena. Often she is asked to explain the meaning and implication of her work to an unbelieving world. She is gracious and uncompromising in her art.

Sitting atop the Blue Ridge mountains near her Asheville, North Carolina, home, Carol dreams of the day when her paintings may adorn the gallery walls of Chicago, New York, or Atlanta. Why? For increased opportunity to tell the secular world of the person and work of the God Incarnate.

The secular media has already taken note. In the recent article, "Professing the Passion of Christianity in Paint," thirty of Carol's paintings are reviewed by the secular press. A newspaper writer exclaims, "C. Bomer professes a vibrant Christian faith in her paintings, but refuses to preach with worn religious imagery. In 'the Unveiling' . . . Bomer explores both her faith and her talents, signing all her work like Bach, Soli Deo Gloria (To God alone the Glory)."

The writer closes the article with the following statements. "Acrylic paint is not a ready medium in which to preach. In her unapologetic art, Bomer bears witness to an inner vision, a faith that cannot be easily put into words, but into images."

Carol demonstrates the power of the gospel communicated in a pagan culture. It is Carol's belief that as Christians our privilege is to embrace excellence in our field so that the world must stop and listen. She quotes Oswald Chambers, "The preacher, lecturer, writer, [painter], must be a man of God first, then a soulful student, that he may write with authority."

Printed over the doorsill of Carol's studio are C. S. Lewis's words paraphrased from *The Weight of Glory:* "No man who values originality will ever be original. But try to tell the Truth as you see it, try to do any bit of work as well as can be done for the glory of God, and what men call originality will come un-sought."

Creativity flourishes in Carol's studio and life as she seeks to use all her talent and expression to reveal, lift up, and glorify Jesus Christ, the Lord of all.

This is Carol's vocation. We can all pause and consider the truth that God will use any yielded vessel to communicate His truth. The resulting possibilities are astounding.

Are you yielding your time, talent, and energy with a desire to articulate the gospel of Jesus Christ to the surrounding world that is groping and searching for answers? God will use any vehicle you offer Him to accomplish this purpose. What offering lies in your hands?

Jana Napoli, in the trendy Warehouse District of New Orleans, is using her God-given talents to reach a growing number of troubled inner-city kids. A successful painter and gallery owner, she came up with an idea as she watched several African-American kids waiting for a bus to take them home from L. E. Rabowin High, a magnet school.

She described her first impression. "One day I looked out the window. I noticed these kids at the bus stop, full of spunk and energy. I saw my neighbors giving them dirty looks." She decided to open her studio to a core group of twenty-five students to train after school in art techniques and marketing skills.

She withdrew $30,000 from her savings account and launched the nonprofit Young Aspiration/Young Artists (YA/YA) program. One teenager, Carlos Neville, looking back on his life before becoming one of Jana's protégés, said, "I used to feel I didn't have a future. Now I realize that I can control where I'm going." Now a fourth-year scholarship student at the School of Visual Arts in New York City, Carlos' future looks like a shining star.

Darlene Francis also sings the praises of YA/YA. She says, "Through YA/YA I learned how to find the things that I want out of life. I learned how to get them, too, not just dream about them."

Jana recalled, "They've been taught all their lives that nobody wants to hear what they have to say. I'm here to show them that people *do* want to listen." Through one woman who recognized a need, fifty teenagers have developed both their artistic skills as well as marketing skills.[1]

Walter Whitman of suburban Chicago is a prime example of a man who is making a difference.

Walter knows about soul food. In a middle-class, suburban Chicago neighborhood, a cosmopolitan brew of Christians—black, white, Asian, and Hispanic—receive a musical feast of African-American soul provided by 120 youthful singers, ages seven through seventeen. They sing, hum, and shout to the clapping of hands.

Walter, classically trained at the Chicago Conservatory of Music, is the minister of music at a racially blended congregation. In 1981 it began as an after-school extracurricular activity that mushroomed into a full-blown musical choir. Walter, a music teacher at Saint John de LaSalle Elementary School, joked, "I didn't even like kids, but God had a different plan."

Requirements to join the "Soul Children" are firm: no drugs, no gang involvement, no teen pregnancies or truancies. Yet hundreds of kids audition for the fewer than thirty openings. Though many of the children don't have a personal relationship with the Lord when they join the choir, Whitman structures the choir to nurture a "total commitment."

He must be succeeding. As their voices ring out, flooding the air with brilliant sound, one singer comments, "We don't just want to sing to people. We want God's Spirit to overflow on them."[2]

Have you heard of the New Harmony project? It is an annual seventeen-day theater and film workshop set in the former Utopian community of New Harmony, Indiana. Eighty actors, writers, directors, and others put in ten-hour days producing a film and rehearsing three plays. Established in 1986, it is a resource network that encourages development of scripts that explore positive human values.

Walter Wangerin, board member and author, explains that the project is not a distinctively Christian endeavor, although a number of Christians comprise the board. Authors throughout the United States submit manuscripts to be considered for the workshop experience. To be selected, the scripts must, in Wangerin's words, "name, celebrate, honor and praise order in the midst of chaos; life in the midst of death; atonement in the midst of separating hatred; liberty in the midst of oppression; sacrifice in the midst of vanity."

According to Thomas S. Giles, "The project's Christian element is not worn on anyone's sleeve, but rather it is delicately woven into New Harmony's fabric—in the plays themselves and in the way they are produced. Many plays get their start here—'Opal,' 'Mama Drama,' 'Johnny Pye,' and 'the Fool-killer' to name a few—have gone on to successful runs in New York, Los Angeles, and other cities; some winning multiple awards. Another play, 'The View from Here,' by Margaret Dulaney opened off-Broadway."[3]

"Right from when I started acting, I knew I never wanted to appear nude on cameras," explains Akosua Busier, actress, playwright, African princess, and daughter of Christian Ashanti, tribal chief in Ghana, Akosua.

"I've always had a rule that I just would not do it, no matter what the price. I've lost roles because of that. I also have a strict rule about cursing. I've been blessed in that. I have taken roles that include cursing in the script and when it gets to those lines, I change them. So far, nobody's challenged me on it. I'll go up to the script girl very quietly and not make a big deal about it, and put something else in place of the curse word."

The actress, best known for her role as "Nettie" in the movie *The Color Purple,* has a strong support group. Frank Wilson, former top Motown music producer, left his position to become a minister. He started a group called "Christian Entertainers' Fellowship." The group comes together to encourage each other."[4]

Finally, Nels and Cynthia Gearing-Marshall are the East Coast regional representatives of the Covenant Players. Created and founded in 1963 by Charles Tanner, the Covenant Players are an international professional religious drama touring ministry. Presently there are over one hundred units on mission in North America, Australia, New Zealand, Europe, Africa, Asia, India, Papua New Guinea, South America, and China. Their sole purpose is to serve Christ.

"Charles Tanner writes about 100 plays each year," Nels explains, "and he is our only writer. After a career of producing films both in the army and in Hollywood, Tanner decided to invest his life in using his talent to help the church. He has written all of the over 1800 plays in the repertoire."

Nels and Cynthia are actors and producers as well as supervisors for the East Coast unit. But they are not alone in their commitment. "We have a core who have been in the Players for many years. There are probably about five hundred people on the road right now," Nels says. "I've been in Players for twenty years, and the East Coast has about twenty-five permanent players."

How are the actors selected? As each unit is on the road, they recruit new members. The person doesn't necessarily have to be a skilled actor, though each is required to be mature, have a positive attitude and good health. The Covenant Players' lifestyle requires stamina, commitment, good character, and the willingness to be a servant after the example of Jesus Christ. Nels explains, "Tanner says that if someone joins because of the acting, they're very serious about that. They'd really get into the characters, and the things that happen to the characters start happening to them. They either quit or changed. We've had several conversions.

"Tanner's focus is on getting folks to act upon the things their lips say. He contends that, without acting, the values you say you believe in just can't mean very much. He feels that the plays' messages (seeds) remain in the heart and minds of people when the actors depart. The local pastor can then nurture and inspire people to bridge the gap between what they say they believe and what they actually do."

These are only a few of scores of people who have found the secret to life investment. Identifying their gifts and skills, they use them daily to invest God's Word in the lives of people, many of whom will join them for eternity.

What are your gifts and talents? Are you using them as a bridge to reach the secular world? Is God using them as a vehicle to communicate His truth through you? He will if you allow Him to. The possibilities are limitless. Don't miss God's opportunity to invest your life where it counts.

———————

Touching Jesus by Touching the World

Have you ever plotted your own personal pilgrimage? Have you identified the Lord's activity in your life to prepare you for investments that count? Stop now to decide how God might be leading you to invest your life in things that matter for eternity.

"Whatever you did for one of the least of these brothers of mine,
you did for me."
Matthew 25:40

What are the rewards for investing your life in things that matter? Not only do you know your days, hours, and moments count for eternity, but you have the privilege of a unique experience with God. You will see Jesus in ways others may never know.

Jesus explained, "Then the righteous will answer Him, 'Lord, when did we see you hungry and feed you, or thirsty and give you something to drink? When did we see you a stranger and invite you in, or needing clothes and clothe you? When did we see you sick or in prison and go to visit you?'

"The King will reply, 'I tell you the truth, whatever you did for one of the least of these brothers of mine, you did for me' (Matt. 25:37–40).

The benefits received from obeying God's words even when it takes us outside our "comfort zone" are incalculable. When was the last time you went beyond ignoring the homeless or moving to the other side of the street? When was the last time you visited a prison? When was the last time you fed a hungry family? When was the last time you gave the unknown UPS man a drink of water?

We do none of these things naturally. Our human nature resists each activity. The power of the Holy Spirit gives us the ability to act supernaturally. Every time you reach out in Jesus' name to touch the life of another, you are reaching out to touch Jesus.

CHARTING YOUR PERSONAL PILGRIMAGE

1. Are you beginning or continuing daily to consider the biblical accuracy of your spoken and unspoken beliefs?

2. Are you developing biblically sharp thinking in the midst of the muddled ideas and philosophies of your world?

3. Are you clear about what you believe? Are there beliefs that need to be eliminated because they have no biblical foundation? Are there others that need to be added which have been previously overlooked?

4. Are you identifying and abandoning the fears that hinder you from pursuing God's will and work in your life?

5. Are you prepared to begin praying that Jesus will equip you to demonstrate attitudes and actions consistent with the biblically sharp thinking you are developing?

6. Does your biblical thinking translate into God-honoring values?

7. How are you growing in your appreciation of the unique person you are becoming in Christ?

8. Do your actions reflect your faith to those who are closest to you?

9. Are you effectively handling the risks of commitment necessary for investment in the will of God?

10. Are you growing in your understanding of secular society so that you can communicate God's Word to your world?

As you consider your personal pilgrimage, the gifts, skills, abilities, and unique experiences known only by you, I've compiled true stories of others who have invested their lives in areas you may have never imagined. My prayer is that one or many will trigger ideas for your future life investment as you complete the days God has given you on this earth.

Long ago, I had a brush with death. John 17:4 became the prayer I wanted to be able to voice to the Father when it was time to meet Him face to face. "Father, I have brought you glory on earth by completing the work you gave me to do." Pray that the Holy Spirit will speak to you as He directs you in new and innovative ways to use the investment of your life for God's kingdom and glory.

NOTES

Chapter 2

1. Stefan Ulstein, "Is Education Going to the Technicians?" *Christianity Today,* 4 September 1987.

Chapter 3

1. Henry Blackaby, *Experiencing God* (Nashville: Broadman & Holman, 1994), 44.
2. Paul Ciotti, "Juries by Nation for No-Fault Violent Crimes," *Richmond Times-Dispatch,* 6 February 1994, sec. F.
3. Malcolm Hill, "Re-establishing a Moral America," May 1991.
4. Susan Jacoby, "Faith, Values & Morals," *McCall's,* May 1989, 69.
5. Robert Holland, "Education and the New Economy," *Richmond Times-Dispatch,* 29 December 1993.
6. Richard Zoglin, "Beyond Your Wildest Dreams," *TIME,* Fall 1992.

Chapter 4

1. Everett Wilson, "Consenting Adults," *Christianity Today*, 29 April 1991, 29.

Chapter 5

1. Cornish Rogers, "On Being Global and Contextual," *Christian Century*, 804.
2. Charles E. Hummel, "Making Friends with Galileo," *Christianity Today*, 11 January 1993.
3. Ibid.
4. Ibid.
5. Louis Moore, "I Could Feel the Presence of God," *Signs of the Times*, February 1990.
6. Ibid.

Chapter 6

1. Ted Ward, *Values Begin at Home* (Victor Books, 1989), 25–26.
2. Patricia LeFever, "Keeping Kids in School, Not in Jail Is Texas Goal," *Nation Magazine*.

Chapter 7

1. August Wilson, *PARADE*.
2. Judith Timson, "Family Value—Not!!," *Chatelane*, 19 January 1993.
3. James Greenlesh, "To China with Love," *Focus on the Family*, April 1992.

Chapter 8

1. Pete Hammond, "On the Job Witnessing That Works," *Christian Herald*, October 1988.
2. Alice Lawson Cox, "Women Like Us Doing the Extraordinary," *VIRTUE*, September/October 1988.
3. Ibid.
4. Hammond, "On the Job Witnessing."

Chapter 9

1. John Crawford, "Christian Business," *WORLD*, 20 January 1990, 10.

Chapter 10

1. Associated Press, "Three-year-old Fighting AIDS," *Asheville Citizen Times*, January 1994.
2. Unknown.
3. Alice Lawson Cox, "Women Like Us, Doing the Extraordinary," *VIRTUE*, September/October 1992.
4. Russell Chandler, "The Changing Church," *Moody*, January 1992, 15.

Chapter 12

1. "Unite and Conquer," *Newsweek*, 5 February 1990.
2. Russell Chandler, *Racing Toward 2001* (Harper Collins, 1992), 292.
3. Ibid.
4. James Rutz, "A New and Better Church," Founders Open Church Ministries, Issue 34.
5. Swift Creek Presbyterian Church "Flyer" (1994).
6. Chandler, *Racing Toward 2001*.

Chapter 13

1. Gretchen Passantino, "Evangelists Find High-Tech Forum," *Moody*, December 1992.
2. Stephen Carter, *The Culture of Disbelief: How American Laws and Politics Trivialize Religious Devotion* (New York: Doubleday, 1994).
3. William Buckley, "God and Man at Yale" reported by James Wall, *Christian Century*, 6 October 1993, 924.
4. James M. Wall, "God as a Hobby," *Christian Century*, 6 October 1993.
5. Patricia Le Fevere, "Media Awkward about Religion—Shun It," *National Catholic Reporter*, 22 October 1993.
6. Ibid.

7. Marian Wright Edelman, *The Measure of Our Success* (Beacon Press, 1992).
8. Anne Reekes, "Get Your School Back on Track," *Parenting*, February 1993.
9. Ruth Dancy, "Women Who Make a Difference," *Family Circle*, 2 November 1993.

Chapter 14

1. Charles Colson, "Being Light in the Darkness," *Discipleship Journal* 72, (1992): 20.
2. Ibid., 21.

Chapter 15

1. Todd Conner, "Is the Earth Alive?" *Christianity Today*, January 1993, 22–24.
2. Ibid., 24.
3. Ibid., 25.
4. Loren Wilkinson, "How Christian Is the Green Agenda?" *Christianity Today*, 11 January 1993, 17.
5. Ronald J. Sider, "Redeeming the Environment," *Christianity Today*, 21 June 1993, 26.
6. Interview with Norm Bomer, editor, World Publications, Asheville, N.C.
7. Ibid.
8. *Smithsonian* magazine, Georgia Pacific, Philips Petroleum, Chemical Manufacturer's Association, May 1995.
9. Calvin B. DeWitt, "Myth #2: It's Not Biblical to be Green," *Christianity Today*, 4 April 1994, 27–28.
10. Loren Wilkerson, "Myth #3: There Is Nothing a Christian Can Do, *Christianity Today*, 4 April 1994, 31–32.
11. DeWitt, "Myth #2."
12. Margaret Jaworski, "They Waste Not," Interview, *Family Circle*, 27 April 1993.
13. Joan Huyser-Honig, "A Green Gathering of Evangelicals," *Christianity Today*, 5 April 1993.
14. Randy Frame, "Greening the Third World," *Christianity Today*, 5 April 1993, 74.

Chapter 16

1. Ruth Lancy, "Women Who Make a Difference," *Family Circle*, 2 November 1993, 19–21.
2. Deward Gilbreath, "The Soul Man," *Christianity Today*, 26 April 1993.
3. Thomas Giles, "High Drama in New Harmony," *Christianity Today*, 11 January 1993, 12.
4. Jerome Shaler, "Science and Society," *US News and World Report*, 20 September 1993, 70.

Sources of Interviews and Questionnaires

Interviews by T. R. Hollingsworth and Linda McGinn

Judson E. "Buddy" Childress, Needle's Eye Ministries (Richmond, Va.)

James Doherty, Loan Assessment Officer, The Fellowship (Richmond, Va.)

Ruth Brinker, Founder and CEO, Fresh Start Farms (San Francisco, Calif.)

Betty Robertson, Speaker and Writer (Roanoke, Va.)

Ken Myers, Executive Producer, Mars Hill Tapes (Powhatan & Charlottesville, Va.)

Nels Gearing-Marshall, Director, Eastern Division, Covenant Players (Richmond, Va.)

Rob Shermerhorn

Joyce Williams

Carol Bomer

Norm Bomer

Scott Holmquist

_____

Questionnaire Responses

Dr. Dennis Hensley (Fort Worth, Tex.)

Holly Miller, Editor, *Saturday Evening Post* (Indianapolis, Ind.)

Linda Beams (Fort Worth, Tex.)

Bob Dowd

LaDonne James

Carole Johnson

Joanne Richards

Marcia Correll

Jennifer Donley

Lana Stephens

Cathy Lowder

Eileen Laso

Tom Hawks

_____

Linda McGinn Waterman is a gifted communicator motivated by a desire to see women develop greater intimacy with God and fulfill His purposes for their lives. Bible teacher, speaker and author, Linda offers women the opportunity to draw near to God, learn to listen to His voice, and catch a glimpse of His face as He reveals Himself through His Word and world. She equips women to be God's ambassadors, His women of purpose "for such a time as this."

Currently working as content developer and curriculum writer for the National Women's Ministry Association, an arm of John Maxwell's Injoy, Linda continues her twenty year experience as a national conference speaker and author of more than 20 books. Linda Waterman's book, *Dancing in the Storm: Hope in the Midst of Chaos* was nominated for the Library of Virginia 2000 Non-Fiction Award. Creator and host of the nationally syndicated radio program, *KeyPoints,* the program received the National Religious Broadcaster's *Genesis Award* in 1994. Her ministry message, "Women of Purpose" brings hope, motivation and encouragement to women. Her organization, "Equipped to Serve" Ministries provides innovative women's ministry solutions that equip women to know God while enabling them to realize their full potential in Christ. Linda McGinn Waterman and her husband, Reen Waterman live in the Annapolis, Maryland area where they share their speaking and writing ministry.

To contact Linda, please write or call:

Equipped to Serve
PO Box 640
Chester, MD 21619
410-490-8083 Phone
Linda@LindaMcGinnWaterman.com

Or visit her web site:
LindaMcGinnWaterman.com

To order additional copies of

INVESTING
YOUR LIFE
IN THINGS
THAT MATTER

Have your credit card ready and call:

1-877-421-READ (7323)

or please visit our web site at
www.pleasantword.com

Also available at: www.amazon.com